WHAT THE **BIBLE** TEACHES ABOUT
# GUIDANCE

WHAT THE **BIBLE** TEACHES ABOUT

# GUIDANCE

Peter Bloomfield

**EP** PUBLISHING WITH A MISSION

EP BOOKS
Faverdale North, Darlington, DL3 0PH, England

**www.epbooks.org**

e-mail: sales@epbooks.org

EP BOOKS USA
P. O. Box 614, Carlisle, PA 17013, USA

**www.epbooks.us**

e-mail: usasales@epbooks.org

First published 2006
*Second impression* 2009

**British Library Cataloguing in Publication Data available**

ISBN-13   978-0-85234-611-2          ISBN 0-85234-611-5

Printed and bound in the United States of America.

*To*
*my wife Lesley*
*whose loving support means everything*

'It is surprising that evangelical Christians, who are so committed to the Bible as God's infallible word, still cling to a subjective view of guidance. In this book Peter Bloomfield challenges readers to show maturity in decision making. They are called on to demonstrate that the Bible sets their thought patterns so that their choices in life are a reflection of the directives that God has given us.

'This book is a very welcome addition to books dealing with the Christian life. It comes from a pastor who has preached through this material, and that orientation of the book makes it particularly useful for others. It sets out clearly the biblical approach, and the questions at the end of each chapter will stimulate further thought.

'Young Christians in particular should be given this book. It will spare them much anguish in trying to reach important decisions — what course of study should I take? Whom should I marry? Where should I buy a house? This book, with its emphasis on the biblical text, the Reformed creeds and the history of the church, will be welcomed by many and widely used.'

Allan M. Harman
*(Emeritus Professor of Old Testament and former principal at the Presbyterian Theological College, Melbourne, Victoria)*

'Today there is much confusion between the authority of Scripture and the authority of the church or that of Christian leaders. John Calvin laboured with no such confusion. He pointed out the crucial difference between the apostles and their successors: "The former were sure and genuine scribes of the Holy Spirit, and their writings are therefore to be considered oracles of God; but the sole office of others is to teach what is provided and sealed in the Holy Scriptures." Peter Bloomfield has sought to apply this necessary insight to some issues raised in modern church life. Hopefully, the result will be greater clarity of thinking, and a more faithful proclamation of gospel truth on the part of the church. This is a most helpful book.'

Peter Barnes
*(Minister of Revesby Presbyterian Church, Sydney, Australia; and teaches Church History at the Presbyterian Theological College in Burwood, NSW)*

# Contents

# 1. How can I know God's will?

*Please read: Psalm 119:97-104*

Of all the issues causing needless stress and confusion among Christians, the question of divine guidance is probably near the top of the list. How can I know God's will for me? What does God want me to do? There is no doubt that God *does* lead and guide his people. 'The LORD is my shepherd … he leads me beside quiet waters … He guides me in paths of righteousness' (Psalm 23). Yes, he leads me, but how can I recognize his leading? Yes, he guides me, but how?

Wherever we are, God guides us: '…if I settle on the far side of the sea, even there your hand will guide me' (Psalm 139:9-10). But again, what does that mean? Does God provide a chatline for regular updates from heaven when we 'log on'? Does God maintain personal communications with millions of individuals throughout history, revealing his will for them in all of life's twists and turns? Are there certain steps we need to learn in order to access information from God that would otherwise be unknown? If so, what are those steps? What is the formula? *How does God guide me?*

Highlighting the importance of this subject, the Bible says, 'those who are led by the Spirit of God are sons of God' (Romans 8:14). In other words, only those people who are being led and guided by God can validly claim to be children of God! So you can see the potential for stress. None of us wants to be a fake Christian. We all want to please God. We want to be confident that we are doing what God wants. But how can we know that?

What is God's will regarding the clothing we wear, the career we follow, and the person we marry? What is God's will regarding my role in the church or sending my children to a private school? History proves that answering these questions can be a daunting matter for many people. Their desire to honour God is good, but they torment themselves needlessly. Why is decision-making so difficult for them? Why is there so much insecurity?

Inevitably the answer lies in various wrong ideas and expectations about 'the will of God'. The problem is a common (traditional) view on guidance that needs to be exposed and discarded. It is helpful to recognize both the wrong approach and the right approach to guidance.

## The wrong approach

This approach begins with the notion of 'God's perfect plan for my life'. Inevitably, guidance then becomes a search for that plan. If such a plan exists it will presumably answer all my questions. It will show 'the perfect centre of God's will for me' in everything. It is assumed that doing God's will always amounts to one possible outcome. There is just one right decision about each issue, one 'centre' of God's will, or one 'perfect plan'. If God's perfect plan for me includes marriage, there is one person at the centre of God's plan, and I must carefully 'discover' the identity of that person. This turns decision-making into a mystery pursuit. Each person becomes a 'detective' trying to solve the mystery of 'discovering God's will'. The assumption is that God leaves a trail of clues and promptings for us to find and fit together like the pieces of a jigsaw puzzle.[1]

The reason this approach is so frustrating is that there is no such thing as 'God's perfect plan for my life'. Scripture does not teach that. Our confidence about doing the will of God does not depend on such an idea. It is also frustrating because it just doesn't work. It is highly subjective. For instance, how do you determine which shoes to wear today? What does God want you to eat for breakfast? What is his perfect plan for the Bible verses you should read today and where to go on holidays? Should you drive to work, or take a bus, a train or a taxi? If God has a perfect plan, then it must include all these things. Inevitably, people become inconsistent, and then, thankfully, ditch such an approach to decision-making. They simply make a free choice based on common sense and personal preference. If they are very pious they may 'baptize' their decisions with a religious mantra such as, 'I felt led to do this, I have a real sense of peace about this.' But the Bible never speaks like that either.

*Illustration*

The wrong approach is captured in the following little story.[2] Imagine Adam and Eve on their first day together. Everything was perfect because there was no sin. After a busy day as the resident horticulturalist in the Garden of Eden, Adam came home to eat the evening meal with his wife. He picked the ingredients from the trees as he walked. While Eve prepared the meal, Adam enjoyed a swim in his personal pool, the Pishon River.

However, things were not so simple in the kitchen. Eve was daunted by the enormity of her task. She was facing too many decisions. She wasn't sure which of the many lovely fruits to serve. She prayed for God's guidance but nothing happened. She knew a choice was unavoidable since they couldn't possibly eat all that abundant supply. She certainly didn't want to miss out on God's perfect will for her at such an early stage of her married life, so she asked Adam to pray on her behalf. 'Please go and ask the Lord what he wants me to prepare for supper.'

Adam did so, but again, nothing happened. He told his wife: 'God didn't give me any new revelation. The only thing we know about his will for our meals is what he said earlier today, namely: "From any tree of the garden you may eat freely; but from the tree of the knowledge of good and evil you shall not eat."' Adam reassured Eve that he had not picked fruit from the forbidden tree.

Eve was still undecided, and no progress was being made with the meal. Adam was ravenous and the crisp red apples were a delight to his eyes. So he said, 'I feel a real sense of peace about them ... I feel led to have apples.' Obligingly, Eve agreed to have apples, hoping the same 'peace' would soon settle upon her. But there was no relief. That decision opened up new problems for Eve. 'Adam, I just can't decide what to do with these apples ... should I slice them, dice them, mash them, bake them in a pie, or prepare cobblers, fritters, dumplings, or apple turnovers; or should we just eat them raw? I want to be very sure of God's will in this matter. I am open to his guiding and leading. I want to be right in the centre of his perfect will for my life. Would you go and ask him for me one more time?'

After praying again, Adam said, 'I got the same answer, "From any tree of the garden you may eat freely, but from the tree of the knowledge of good and evil you shall not eat."' After a time of silent reflection, Adam said, 'You know, Eve, the Lord made this statement as though it should fully answer my question — I'm sure he could have told me exactly what to eat and how to eat it, but I think he wants us to make those decisions ... just like naming the animals today, he left that up to me.'

Eve was stunned but relieved: 'Do you mean that it doesn't matter which of these fruits we have for supper or how I prepare them? Are you telling me that I cannot possibly miss God's will in this decision? Are you telling me that God has not left me to tortuously "discover" every detail of his perfect plan for my life before I act?'

Then they both adopted the same wise conclusion: 'The only way you could miss God's will is to eat from the forbidden tree. But he has given us a wide range of liberty ... all the other fruits are in his will. To make godly decisions we simply need to exercise our freedom and obey everything God has told us. So let's have fruit salad!'

See the problem? Eve acted as if life was a mysterious journey searching for just one exclusively correct choice at the 'centre of God's will'. She didn't understand the vast range of liberty God has given us in decision-making. The 'will of God' is not just one small dot in the centre of a circle. Rather, it is usually a vast ocean of possibilities where hundreds or thousands of alternative choices are pleasing to God. *So long as we act according to the Word of God we are free to decide as we wish.* Therein lies the problem! Many Christians cannot cope with freedom.

> **Believers want God to spoon-feed them like babies... In fact God ... gives us broad principles to work with and he expects us to use them.**

## A shocking truth

Believers are generally more at ease with endless rules than broad liberty. They prefer immaturity to wisdom. They want God to spoon-feed them like babies, giving them every detail, virtually making each decision for them. In fact God treats us like mature adults. He gives us broad principles to work with and he expects us to use them as we freely choose among many legitimate options.

## The right approach

There is no point asking if a particular event is according to 'the will of God' because that is a very ambiguous term. It has two completely distinct meanings. The right approach to guidance begins by recognizing that distinction. God's will is either *revealed* or *unrevealed*. The following diagram will assist our thinking.

## God's will

**Revealed will**
His commands
Moral will
Precepts
*(What should happen)*

**Secret will**
His plan
Sovereign will
Decrees
*(What will happen)*

- **God's revealed will** (on the left of the diagram)

This is also called God's *moral will* or God's *preceptive will*. It refers to what God has plainly said, what he expects and demands from all people. It describes what is right and wrong, what is pleasing and displeasing to him. It consists of all the ethical principles God wants to shape all our thoughts, words and deeds ... all our working, resting, eating, drinking, rising up, lying down, buying and selling.

God has told us his moral will. It is written down for all to see in sixty-six books of Scripture. It is outlined in the Ten Commandments (Exodus 20), and summarized further in two broad principles: 'Love the Lord your God with all your heart and with all your soul and with all your mind ... Love your neighbour as yourself' (Matthew 22:36-40). When we act in accordance with those principles we are doing God's will. We are making good decisions. So God's revealed will teaches us what *should* happen and what *should not* happen.

- **God's unrevealed will** (on the right of the diagram)

God's unrevealed will is also called his *sovereign will, secret will,* or *covenant will.* Another term is God's *decretive will* since it refers to everything he has eternally decreed. It is God's master plan for everything in the universe. It is his blueprint of what will definitely come to pass throughout history. It includes everything that happens — when and how and why it happens — and how God will use it all for his own glory as he fulfils his covenant oath. In this secret will, God so rules and overrules in the decisions freely made by men and angels that God's ultimate purposes come to pass. This means that all things will be subject to Christ as King of kings. We need to grasp several facts about this secret will of God.

*a. We cannot know it until after it happens*

If you want to know what is God's sovereign will for your life tomorrow morning, you'll have to wait until tomorrow afternoon. Then you will know it. Whatever did happen that morning was ordained in God's secret purposes and decrees. We do not and cannot know what God has in store for us in the future. Nowhere does God have a separate third 'will' called 'a perfect plan for your life'. The map of your life is just one detail among billions of details in his sovereign (secret) will. God does not expect you to know that map with all its twists and turns. When people are looking for that sort of guidance they will be frustrated. God does not give it. We only know it from hindsight.

Moses sums it up in Deuteronomy 29:29: 'The secret things belong to the LORD our God, but the things revealed belong

16

to us and to our children for ever, that we may follow all the words of this law.' In other words, there is a secret will of God, but these secret things are none of our business: 'The secret things belong to the LORD our God.' We have all the guidance we need in Scripture, namely, 'the things revealed ... all the words of this law'. That *is* our business! That *is* for us and our children to observe constantly. That *is* how we make good decisions. Everything the Bible explicitly teaches and logically implies is the entire will of God for us. As long as we make decisions consistent with the Bible we are acting rightly. That is the only indication of God's will that we need.

b. *It wouldn't help if we knew it!*

There would be no advantage in being able to pry into God's sovereign will, because you cannot possibly miss out on it anyway. It is impossible to avoid or frustrate what God has secretly purposed and decreed. Moreover, it would be very confusing and counterproductive if God did reveal his sovereign plan for your life. Why? Because it includes your sins and mistakes! His sovereign will includes all our moral and immoral actions. It includes all our good and evil deeds. So it includes many things that actually displease God and violate his moral will. God's secret will includes all the perversity and unbelief of all men and angels in all of history.

It includes the sin of Adam, the murder of Christ and the cruelty inflicted upon martyrs burned at the stake. It must include all these things because God is in control. Nothing happens except he ordained it. What use would it be if God revealed his secret will? It only indicates what you *will* do, not what you *should* do.

17

Suppose you find that tomorrow at 3.00pm, in God's sovereign purpose, you are going to say certain things. That's no help or guidance because you need to know if you *should* say those things. Again we come back to the only guidance needed, the moral will of God (especially Scripture's teaching on the use of the tongue). The Bible is our sufficient guide for all of life's decisions. 'All Scripture is God-breathed and is useful for teaching, rebuking, correcting and training in righteousness, so that the man of God may be thoroughly equipped for every good work' (2 Timothy 3:16-17).

Remember! Nobody is judged for failing to obey God's sovereign will, not even the devil! Nobody can possibly disobey it! Not even Satan is capable of doing something God has not purposed in his master plan. Everyone will be judged by God's revealed moral will.

> Nobody is judged for failing to obey God's sovereign will, not even the devil! Nobody can possibly disobey it! Not even Satan is capable of doing something God has not purposed in his master plan.

The Bible provides principles of conduct affecting every aspect of life, adequately equipping us for every good work. But it must be interpreted in the right way. It is all too easy to act incorrectly due to misreading the Bible. In later chapters we will consider how to avoid errors of interpretation. We will also consider where prayer fits in, and the role of logical reasoning. For now, we will look at two examples of how the Apostles acted when making decisions.

*1 Thessalonians 3*

Paul had started the church in Thessalonica. Later, in Athens, he realized that the Thessalonican Christians were about to suffer a period of persecution. He was especially concerned that they had no experienced leaders. So Paul and Silas made a decision: 'So when we could stand it no longer, we thought it best to be left by ourselves in Athens. We sent Timothy, who is our brother and God's fellow worker in spreading the gospel of Christ, to strengthen and encourage you in your faith, so that no one would be unsettled by these trials' (1 Thessalonians 3:1-3).

Notice how they made their decision: 'we thought it best'. They made a wise and rational decision, consistent with God's moral will. They did not try to determine 'God's perfect plan'. They did not receive any revelations or divine promptings. Paul does not say, 'We felt led to send Timothy', the type of mystical language so many use today. They carefully weighed up all the options and did what seemed best.

*Philippians 2*

Epaphroditus had come from Philippi to visit Paul in prison at Rome. He became ill to the point of nearly dying, but God restored him. Paul then made a decision to send him home because the Philippians were distressed to hear of his sickness and Epaphroditus was missing them too. 'But I think it is necessary to send back to you Epaphroditus... For he longs for all of you and is distressed because you heard he was ill' (Philippians 2:25-26). Paul made this decision *not* because he had been directed by God to do so, *not* because he 'felt led', and *not* because he had looked for a sign or 'put out a fleece' to know God's leading as Gideon had done (see Judges 6:36-40). He simply decided that it was wise and necessary in the circumstances. We too are to act wisely and biblically as mature moral agents.

This is the right approach to guidance. Paul certainly prayed about his decisions, but he was not asking God to show his secret will. Prayer asks for wisdom, so that we can discern the circumstances well and set the priorities wisely. Prayer also seeks God's blessing on our decisions, and confesses our humble dependence on him. The outworking and success of every decision depends on God. Unless the Lord builds the house they labour in vain.

## Questions

1. *How do the following texts prove that God in his 'sovereign will' can even use things that violate his 'moral will'? (Genesis 50:20; Daniel 3:15-30; Matthew 26:21-25; Acts 2:23-24.)*

2. *'According to Galatians 2:11-21 even the apostle Peter found liberty hard to handle.' Do you agree or disagree with that comment, and why?*

3. *Explain how the true principles of guidance are well summed up in Isaiah 8:19-20.*

# 2. How God guides us

*Please read: Psalm 119:105-112*

> Guide me, O Thou great Jehovah,
> Pilgrim through this barren land;
> I am weak, but Thou art mighty,
> Hold me with Thy powerful hand.

So we sing and so we believe. We want God to guide us and we believe he does; but *how?* The answer lies in the distinction between God's *revealed will* and his *secret will*. That means there are two forms of guidance. God's revealed will amounts to 'upfront' guidance, while his secret will amounts to 'behind the scenes' guidance. It will be useful to consider each of these, along with some illustrations.

1. Guidance 'upfront'
2. Guidance 'behind the scenes'
3. Guidance illustrated

## Guidance 'upfront'

To read the Bible is to experience God's candid 'upfront' guidance. Right there in 'hard copy' God declares his mind, telling us his will on every conceivable human action and motive. There he tells us what should and should not happen in the world. This 'upfront' guidance is summarized in the Ten Commandments, and focused in the two great principles of loving our God and our neighbour. On top of that, the Bible provides numerous detailed examples in myriads of people and events, together with God's associated judgements, approvals, disapprovals, rebukes and warnings.

> The Bible is not a textbook on mathematics, medicine, engineering or law. But it does sufficiently provide the ethical rules for judging what is morally right and morally wrong in every field.

God's 'upfront' guidance is his unchanged and unchangeable word, the Bible. It is utterly reliable and sufficient to prepare us for every good work and every good decision that life requires. In the Bible we have all the guidance needed for honouring God in our daily life. We lack nothing. However, this 'sufficiency of Scripture' must not be taken out of context. It does not mean that the Bible provides encyclopaedic information on every topic under the sun. But it does show man what is necessary to be right with God and to live right with God.

It is important to remember that the Bible is not a textbook on mathematics, medicine, engineering or law. It is not sufficient for instruction on how to fly planes, perform surgery, or conduct electricity. But it does sufficiently provide the ethical rules for judging what is morally right and morally wrong in every field. The Bible is sufficient for us to mark out the true limits of human freedom in medicine and mathematics, production and politics, aeronautics and the arts. There is no corner of the universe where the light of God's Word does not penetrate with its holy judgements.

## Guidance 'behind the scenes'

Paul expresses this beautifully: 'God causes all things to work together for good to those who love God, to those who are called according to his purpose' (Romans 8:28, NASB). From our human perspective, God is working 'behind the scenes', bringing about good results that would not naturally occur. His purposes will stand because he rules and overrules all things. Of course we are usually unaware of it happening. What we do experience can be so unpleasant that it feels like God has actually lost control. It may feel like nothing is working for our good. Job didn't know what God was doing behind the scenes, nor did Jeremiah in the pit, nor Joseph in prison, nor Jonah drowning in the Mediterranean. Yet the Bible asserts divine control. God is mysteriously and providentially guiding his people. It is just one aspect of his sovereignty, by which all events happen according to his predetermined plan and counsel.

This 'behind the scenes' guidance is quite unpredictable because it allows many things to happen which God's 'upfront' guidance says should not happen. God tells us 'up front' not to cheat, or murder, or steal, or tell lies, or covet. But God incorporates those immoral things into his 'behind the scenes' guidance (secret will). They happen, but God rules and overrules them as he pleases, for the glory of his name and the blessedness of his chosen people. Moreover, there is no standard rule for predicting *how* God will guide and govern the course of history. Such information is not available for our daily decision-making.

Of course, it is right and appropriate to trust in God's 'behind the scenes' guidance. It is good to pray and sing 'Guide me, O Thou great Jehovah ... Hold me with Thy powerful hand.' Spiritual maturity depends on that. It is vital to know that even when we get things wrong, God is behind the scenes ruling and guiding so that our ultimate good is achieved. But, as Moses insisted, God does not tell us the steps in that process: 'The secret things belong to the LORD our God' (Deuteronomy 29:29). Our duty is to listen to God's 'upfront' guidance and walk by that light alone. While God's secret will comforts and reassures us, only his revealed will can guide our decisions. This distinction between 'upfront' and 'behind the scenes' guidance can be seen with a few texts.

*Some 'upfront' texts*

'I will instruct you and teach you in the way you should go; I will counsel you and watch over you' (Psalm 32:8). In the book of Psalms God's counsel, teaching and instructing refers to the Torah (the Mosaic writings). It consists of the precepts, commands, judgements and statutes given to Israel. We see it again as a question and answer: 'How can a young man keep his way pure? By living according to your word' (Psalm 119:9).

And again, 'Your word is a lamp to my feet and a light for my path. I have taken an oath and confirmed it, that I will follow your righteous laws' (Psalm 119:105-106). So Scripture guides us by shining its light on the path we should walk in. Psalm 1 is also a classic expression of 'upfront' guidance. Who is the blessed man? 'His delight is in the law of the LORD, and on his law he meditates day and night' (v. 2). What is his conviction? 'Send forth your light and your truth, let them guide me; let them bring me to your holy mountain, to the place where you dwell' (Psalm 43:3).

*Some 'behind the scenes' texts*

In words repeated by Christ on the cross, the psalmist knows that God is guiding behind the scenes: 'Since you are my rock and my fortress, for the sake of your name lead and guide me. Free me from the trap that is set for me, for you are my refuge. Into your hands I commit my spirit' (Psalm 31:3-5). He trusts the God who overrules every evil plot that would destroy his people.

'Before I was afflicted I went astray, but now I obey your word ... It was good for me to be afflicted so that I might learn your decrees' (Psalm 119:67, 71). David admits that he had been sinning by ignoring the 'upfront' guidance of God. But God was at work 'behind the scenes'. He providentially brought sickness or some other affliction to cause the writer to see the folly of his ways, returning obediently to the guidance of God's Word.

## Guidance illustrated

The three following individual illustrations — relating to Joni Eareckson, disobedience in marriage, and setting up shop — provide useful examples of how the two forms of guidance operate.

*Joni Eareckson*

Millions have read her story. At seventeen years of age this healthy young Christian girl was instantaneously changed into a quadriplegic. It was 30 July 1967 at Chesapeake Bay. Joni dived into shallow water, broke her neck and remains paralysed from the neck down. It changed the course of her whole life. Was this God 'guiding' her? Was God making her paths straight and causing all things to work together for her good?

Yes, but she didn't think so then. It certainly didn't feel like it. But in her books[1] Joni assures us that behind the scenes God was carrying out his mighty purposes in guiding her! At the time of the accident Joni had no knowledge of God's secret will for her. It could never have come into her decision-making and planning. Who knows what Joni had planned for the following day, 31 July 1967? Who knows what she had written in her diary? One thing is sure: she had not written 'go and lie in a hospital Stryker Frame as a quadriplegic'!

The plans she had made for the days, weeks and years ahead may all have been good. They may all have been consistent with God's 'upfront' guidance. Yet suddenly they were all overruled from 'behind the scenes'. Such divine guidance is totally unpredictable, totally secret, totally sovereign and sometimes very unpalatable! Even when we make good decisions, God is not bound to facilitate them!

Mark this well! God declares: 'As the heavens are higher than the earth, so are my ways higher than your ways and my thoughts than your thoughts' (Isaiah 55:9). That is true even when we act correctly. God's ways are higher than even our right and proper ways. He is not obliged to endorse our good decisions. He often does, but sometimes he does not! Since he remains King of heaven and earth, he may guide us into other paths for his own glory and our ultimate good. True humility depends on joyfully recognizing this fact.

> That God's ways are higher than our ways and his thoughts than our thoughts is true even when we act correctly... True humility depends on joyfully recognizing this fact.

As a quadriplegic Joni has accomplished far more for the kingdom of God than she could ever have done as an able-bodied person. Her books reveal how she overcame her struggles with depression and questioning God's love and wisdom. Her story is a gospel triumph of grace.

The point is that since the accident has changed her life, Joni makes different decisions. She had to cross out of her diary that canoe-trip, that basketball game, that school dance, and that cross-country run. She now knows more of the 'behind the scenes guidance' of God, but only after it has happened. She still makes all her decisions based on the 'upfront' guidance of God (Scripture) but her range of options has changed. The lesson for us is clear.

Our journey through life is a mysterious interconnection between two things. On one side are all the decisions we make in the light of God's upfront guidance. They will be a mixture of good, bad and indifferent decisions. On the other side, our life depends on what God does 'behind the scenes' with all these decisions. He will rule and overrule them according to his glorious wisdom. But we cannot know anything about that until after it occurs. In the meantime, we must keep making common-sense decisions consistent with Scripture. In that way we are right in the centre of God's will.

## Disobedience in marriage

To illustrate the danger of making decisions based on what God sometimes does 'behind the scenes', consider a Christian girl wanting to marry. God's 'upfront' guidance is quite clear. She is free to marry any consenting man as long as he is a Christian, not already married, and not a close blood relative.

But she is keen on a non-Christian, and she knows the Bible says she should only marry a Christian. She knows God says, 'Do not be yoked together with unbelievers. For what do righteousness and wickedness have in common? Or what fellowship can light have with darkness?' (2 Corinthians 6:14). But she recalls other cases like hers. She knows about another Christian who knowingly disobeyed God and married an unbeliever, but God graciously converted him too. The husband came to faith in Christ and now both of them are true believers. Encouraged by this case of God's 'behind the scenes' guidance, she disobeys Scripture and marries the non-Christian. How should we assess such things?

28

Firstly, this clinging to the 'behind the scenes' mercy of God is very selective. Yes, sometimes God does convert the non-Christian spouse, but often he does not. It is quite unpredictable. Why wasn't she guided by the hurt and misery evident in other disobedient marriages? In any case we must not put God to the test. It is very presumptive. Paul's outcry needs repeating: 'Shall we go on sinning, so that grace may increase? By no means!' (Romans 6:1).

Secondly, you can never justify any sin on the grounds that God might bring some good out of it! Yes he might, but that is motivation for praising God, not repeating the sin! Thirdly, the argument is contradictory. It amounts to saying: 'I'm going to be ungodly in order to make someone else godly … I'm going to displease God in the hope that he might be pleased to bless me.' So again, the only guidance we must act upon in all our decisions is the revealed will of God.

*Setting up shop*

'Now listen, you who say, "Today or tomorrow we will go to this or that city, spend a year there, carry on business and make money." Why, you do not even know what will happen tomorrow. What is your life? You are a mist that appears for a little while and then vanishes. Instead, you ought to say, "If it is the Lord's will, we will live and do this or that." As it is, you boast and brag. All such boasting is evil. Anyone, then, who knows the good he ought to do and doesn't do it, sins' (James 4:13-17).

What point is James making? He certainly is not saying that setting up shop to make a profit is wrong. Rather, he is warning against *presumption*, the attitude that ignores the fact that God may not fulfil even perfectly legitimate plans. The Bible agrees with free enterprise and reasonable profit. God's 'upfront' revelation is all we need to guide us in how we should behave if we decide to go into business.

But we must never forget that God controls the whole outcome. We may not even be alive tomorrow, let alone profiting in business! We need no more than the Bible to guide us, but we must never make decisions without reckoning on God's sovereign purposes beyond the Bible ('behind the scenes'). He may have other purposes. Let that always be the bottom line.

## Conclusion

Every one of us has many decisions to make. Will I change my old car yet? Will I try for a different job? Will we have another child? Should I expand the existing house or buy a bigger one? What subjects will I study at university next year? It is encouraging to know that God leaves you 100% free to choose *what you want!* So long as it is consistent with what he says 'up front', you are free! Use your common sense to weigh up the options — and then do it!

But remember — you will be guided from behind the scenes! God is at work causing all his wise purposes to be achieved. You cannot sense it or identify it, but you can rely on it. Blessed be God who so wondrously and graciously provides and guides.

## Questions

1. *How do the following texts show that not even Satan can disobey God's decretive will? (Proverbs 16:4; Jude 6; 2 Peter 2:2-22.)*

2. *'While God's sovereign will made sin certain it provides no excuse for sinners.' Assess that using 2 Corinthians 5:10; Romans 1:18-20; & 2:12-16.*

3. *How is the revealed will of God a sufficient guide against temptation (Luke 4:1-13) and a sufficient guide for life (Matthew 7:21-27)?*

4. *What is implied about guidance in Philippians 1:9-10?*

# 3. Making good decisions

*Please read: Proverbs 3:5-6*

God wants all our decisions to be common-sense applications of all he has explicitly said and logically implied in the Bible. That doesn't mean decision-making is simply a clinical matter of rationality, leaving no place for prayer and faith. Good decision-making involves an important interplay of prayer, reason and faith. But what is the connection between them? To clarify how they fit together, Proverbs 3:5-6 is a convenient focal point: 'Trust in the LORD with all your heart and lean not on your own understanding; in all your ways acknowledge him, and he will make your paths straight.' What does that mean?

1. The role of prayer
2. The role of reason
3. The role of faith

## The role of prayer

If good decision-making comes from knowing the Bible and acting accordingly, why pray? What exactly should we pray for? Though prayer is very important, not all prayers about guidance honour God. Some prayers virtually deny the sufficiency of Scripture! The denial may be unintentional and unconscious, but it is real. It happens when people pray for God to provide new revelation. It happens when God is asked to personally 'speak to my heart' about what decision to take. Not only is this asking God to spoon-feed us like babies, but it also embraces the idea of 'ongoing revelation', an error emphatically denied in the historic Christian creeds (see chapter 8 for more details).

Regardless of the exact words used, prayer should never amount to asking for some extra guidance outside of Scripture. Such prayer does not really believe that Scripture alone is sufficient 'so that the man of God may be thoroughly equipped for every good work' (2 Timothy 3:17). So what is the role of prayer? What should we pray for? Four things need to be emphasized.

Firstly, we pray for *a right interpretation of Scripture*. 'Lord, help me to gather up the biblical teachings in context, in harmony and in proportion. Give me a right understanding of Scripture as it relates to the decision I need to make.' We pray for the illumination of the Holy Spirit so that we will interpret each part of Scripture in harmony with the whole. We don't want to twist or distort God's Word by ignoring the context and literary genre. We don't want to be a victim of ignorance, so we pray for a teachable spirit that will listen to teachers with proven competence in Christian orthodoxy.

Secondly, we pray for the *wisdom and discernment* needed for correctly assessing all the circumstances of the decision. We need wisdom to keep things in proportion, to set correct priorities and to avoid majoring on minors. We need wisdom both to deal with the opinions and reactions of others, and to know how to handle the possible consequences of our decision. We need wisdom to know which of any valid alternatives will be the most expedient, useful and practical.

Thirdly, we pray for the *humility and spiritual discipline* to be submissive to Scripture, especially when it goes 'against the grain'. Godliness involves self-denial. Options that might personally suit us will sometimes have a detrimental effect on others. We pray for God to give us the grace to know when self-denial is appropriate. Whenever we put the interests of the kingdom of God first, there is a cost. Regardless of our personal interests, each of us needs to ask questions like: *What is the best decision for my family? How will it affect my usefulness and availability in the church?* We also need humility after a decision is made. No matter how wise and biblical the decision was, the results may be very different to our expectations. God is not bound to 'join the dots' according to our mental projections.

Fourthly, we pray that we will recognize *God's sovereign rights*. He is perfectly free to bless or hinder our plans as he sees fit. Like Jesus, we need to pray, 'Not my will but yours be done.' Therefore we pray for grace to love God no matter what he does with our decision. If he is pleased to prosper it, let us give him all the glory. Should he bring it to nothing, or even bring chastisement and affliction along with it, let us respond with the humility of Job: 'The Lord gives, and the Lord takes away: blessed be the name of the Lord.' In other words, prayer expresses our desire to let God be God. We pray that the master of the universe would do whatever he wishes with everything in this universe, including our decisions and plans.

That is the meaning of Proverbs 3:6: 'in all your ways acknowledge him'. Acknowledge God as the sovereign ruler, and acknowledge his right to rule as he deems fit. Acknowledge him as perfect wisdom, virtue and knowledge. Don't be annoyed if your good decisions on earth are overruled by better decisions from heaven. These are the right ways to pray about guidance.


## The role of reason

Reason refers to rational thinking (God-given common sense). Two extreme views need to be avoided.

One view *minimizes* reason, denying reason its legitimate place. Such people take the naive and dangerous view that the Bible can be interpreted without strict attention to any formal rules arising from context, or grammar, or linguistics. As a result, proper principles of interpretation are ignored. These people trample over the important differences between poetic, proverbial, parabolic, hyperbolic, apocalyptic and typological literature. They see every Bible verse on a 'dead level' plane, treating it all as narrative prose, and taking everything as literally as possible.

Sadly, there is a mindless form of Christianity that opposes careful, scholarly, rational exegesis of Scripture. It is manifested by those who counsel sick people to 'throw away the pills ... there's no need for medicine or doctors ... faith is sufficient ... there's healing in the atonement, so "Name it and claim it!"'

The opposite extreme *maximizes* the place of reason. This is 'rationalism', making human reason supreme. Anything that cannot be proved by 'reason' is regarded as spurious. It leads people to deny such clear Bible truths as the Virgin Birth of Christ, his resurrection from the dead, and miracles, on the grounds that they cannot be proved by reason.

Beware of ignoring history! There is an unhealthy individualism in our age that ignores the marvellous testimony of orthodox Christianity over 2000 years. When human reason produces doctrines contrary to those embodied in the great creeds of the church, alarm bells should ring. When the most eminent champions of the faith have repeatedly defended the gospel against perversions in every age, we are wise to stand with them. Had that been done, neither of these abuses of 'reason' could have endured.

Consider the meaning of the command: 'Lean not on your own understanding' (Proverbs 3:5). This text rejects both extreme views noted above. It rejects the minimalist error. The text does not say, 'Do not use your understanding ... do not apply rational argument ... do not use your brain.' And it rejects rationalism. The text says, 'Do not rest on human logic, do not make it your ultimate rule; do not put all your weight upon it! Instead, put all your trust in God who rules and overrules all human decisions.' There are always gaps in our knowledge. We

> When the most eminent champions of the faith have repeatedly defended the gospel against perversions in every age, we are wise to stand with them.

cannot see into the future. There are unknown factors. There is mystery in providence. That is true even after 'providence' occurs, let alone beforehand. Even the most logical decisions have to allow for some unpredictable factors. So the proper role of reason involves several tasks.

Firstly, reason uses Scripture sensibly. Some people derive incorrect guidance from Scripture because they either interpret or apply it wrongly. They ignore the grammatical, historical, literary and contextual factors in Scripture. The proper use of reason produces interpretations that systematically harmonize with the entire Bible. Then reason applies those interpretations correctly to the decisions of life. It is appalling to see good scholarship being treated with disdain and contempt among some professing Christians.

Secondly, reason allows for unpredictable factors. Reason has a fallback position wherever possible, a 'Plan B'. It provides for the 'what if' factor. Reason has a role to play *after* we make the decision, especially when things didn't work out as expected. Even then, 'Lean not on your own understanding'! Don't be too sure that you have interpreted the results correctly. A result that appears disastrous to human understanding may not be so. We have all seen, with hindsight, that seemingly catastrophic events have, in the providence of God, been for the good of others and ourselves.

Thirdly, reason handles freedom properly. Reason is especially important where we have the most freedom in making decisions, where Scripture gives us many options. For instance, a Christian is free to buy any house on the market. Because there are literally millions of legitimate options, 'reason' will have a leading role in making the decision.

These sorts of decisions are not matters of 'right or wrong' but 'good or better'. Reason will weigh up several important issues. Can I afford a house of this high quality? Should I buy an average house I can easily afford or a better one that will stretch my budget? Is this house only cheap because it 'suits the handyman' (namely, an experienced builder with a great deal of time, money and expertise)?

Reason considers the wisdom of buying a house in the country as opposed to a suburban home close to work and school. Is it reasonable to buy 'a home in the bush' if I suffer from hay fever? A multi-storey dwelling is good for space, but what if I have a heart problem or arthritis? Can I cope with all the stairs? So the role of reason is important because the Bible gives us a large area of liberty in decision-making. If there was just one right decision, just one exact 'centre of God's will', 'reason' is marginalized and has very little to do. You just search for the needle in the haystack until you find it!

## The role of faith

Faith means trust, belief, or confidence. It plays a very significant role in decision-making. We need faith in Scripture as the infallible Word of God. We need faith that God is always in control. But with some people faith spills over its banks to become sheer presumption. People put faith in things they have no right to. They have trusts and beliefs that are unwise and unwarranted.

Assume for a moment that a wise and prayerful decision has been made. We know the decision was sensible. All the other options had undesirable consequences (including doing nothing or procrastinating). Now that our conscience is clear and the decision is made, *what is the role of faith?* What are we entitled to believe about our decision? In general terms the answer is summed up in Proverbs 3:6: 'and he will make your paths straight'. But we need to be clear about what that does and does not mean.

It certainly does not mean *plain sailing,* sunny days and blue skies. You are not entitled to believe that the outcome of any decision will be trouble free. It is not an article of faith. When Christians act 100% biblically, it often brings serious troubles upon them. It did so for Daniel, it did for Jesus, and it did for the Apostles and martyrs. The right road may be a rough and difficult road, but so long as it is the right road we must travel it. Christianity is not an easy life. Seeking the interests of the kingdom of God does not relieve us of troubles. Making good decisions does not cause Satan to fly the white flag and surrender! The only boat that never experiences rough water is the one in dry dock.

> The right road may be a rough and difficult road, but so long as it is the right road we must travel it.

Nor does it mean *peace.* We are not entitled to believe that good decisions leave us free of doubts. It is wrong to think that if you have acted by all the right rules then you'll finish up with 'a real sense of peace' about it, a conviction and assurance that this is the right path. Some people think that until this feeling of peace and certainty comes, a decision is premature, and you should keep praying and waiting. This is not the case.

Sometimes certainty is possible because Scripture leaves no options about a decision (should I steal that car?). But most decisions are more complex and we cannot be sure of being on 'the right path'. Often there is an element of uncertainty and that is healthy if it causes a genuine trust in God. It is somewhat misleading to translate the text as 'He will *direct* your path' … as if God is like an officer directing traffic exactly where to turn, where to stop, and where to go.

To understand what Proverbs 3:6 means, the New Testament has a very helpful definition of faith: 'Now faith is being sure of what … we do not see' (Hebrews 11:1). What is it that we cannot see (concerning this topic of guidance)? We cannot see how God is guiding 'behind the scenes'! We cannot see the secret will of God. But we believe it implicitly! Faith is utterly convinced that God will rule and overrule in all our decisions. Genuine obedience to God will not ultimately bring us to grief. The assurance that God makes our paths 'straight' obviously implies that they need straightening! There are some crooked bits, some twists and turns. If they are not straightened out they will harm us. Faith knows that God will remove all ultimate harm by straightening our paths. Our best decisions are imperfect, but God will use them to his glory and for our sanctification.

The role of faith is to believe that 'God causes all things to work together for good for those who love him, who are the called according to his purpose' (Romans 8:28, NASB). Even our unwise decisions, our hasty and ignorant decisions, are all accounted for in God's sovereign will (his 'behind the scenes' guidance). He knows how to make them turn out for our good and his glory. It is faith's role to believe that! In that general sense a Christian does have a constant sense of 'peace' and deliverance from paranoia.

It is very comforting to know that if you honour God, he will honour you. As you 'trust in the Lord with all your heart and in all your ways acknowledge him', God causes all your ways to work together for good. They may not be good in themselves, but they are not by themselves. God mixes them with everything else so that good ultimately results!

God does not promise that we will be conscious of this happening. On the contrary, his ruling and overruling takes place behind the scenes. We cannot see how he makes our paths straight. It can all look very mysterious to us. You cannot feel that everything now happening to you is being worked for your good. Did Daniel feel that his path was 'straight' in the lion's den? But faith rises above feelings! Faith embraces what is not yet seen. Faith believes that God is true to his promises.

While the proper functioning of prayer, reason and faith is critical for legitimate decision-making, it does not end there. Good decision-making is more complex than correctly recognizing the scope of biblical freedom. In the interests of other people, self-denial may be involved in the choices we make. Legitimacy has to be weighed against factors like expediency and neighbourly love (see chapter 14 for more details and examples). Nothing written here suggests that guidance is a simple mechanical procedure.

## Questions

1. *'In his heart a man plans his course, but the LORD determines his steps' (Proverbs 16:9). How should this affect our concept of 'guidance'?*

2. *'By faith Abraham, when called to go to a place he would later receive as his inheritance, obeyed and went, even though he did not know where he was going' (Hebrews 11:8). Identify the main features of 'guidance' here.*

3. *'Abraham reasoned that God could raise the dead, and, figuratively speaking, he did receive Isaac back from death' (Hebrews 11:19). How does this illustrate the proper use of human reason?*

# 4. God sends no e-mails!

*Please read: Psalm 119:1-16*

'It is more dangerous to tread on the corns of a live giant than to cut off the head of a dead one: but it is more useful and better fun' (C. S. Lewis). What I am about to say will no doubt tread on the corns of a giant; but it is certainly not done lightly (for 'fun'). It is unavoidable, intended to make him face reality. The 'giant' to which I refer is the global church that has adopted an unreal language, 'God-talk'. It is full of clichés and stock phrases that serve as 'sacred' (pompous) ways of saying something fairly ordinary.

When the giant has an idea, he never calls it an idea. He goes to his 'God-talk' dictionary and uses much more spiritual phrases like: 'I have a vision', 'I have a burden', or 'The Lord laid it on my heart.' Rather than describe his daily walk as 'doing what the Bible says', he uses the mysterious term, 'being open to the leading of the Spirit'. Since the giant still does not know what this means, he uses even more 'God-talk' to explain it as 'the anointing of the Spirit' or 'the unction of the Spirit'. There is some neat 'God-talk' to cover everything, but it is especially noticeable in reference to the topic of guidance. Christians often baptize their decisions with 'God-talk'. For example, 'I felt led' or 'the Lord led me to do this' are very common expressions today. When you ask how this 'leading' took place you learn that various circumstances, events and experiences have been interpreted as little *messages* from God. People assume that God is dropping hints about his will for their life, and they read it like an e-mail from heaven.

This is wrong and dangerous. *God sends no e-mails!* I am not disputing that God controls the providential circumstances around us. Yes he does, but they are *not* 'messages' or 'signs' from God. They are not little hints being dropped from heaven. They are not little previews into God's secret will. I am acutely aware how deeply entrenched is the opposite view. It is virtually a 'sacred cow', and any opinion to the contrary is most unwelcome. It is treading on corns! But I urge you to think objectively. What I am about to tell you will stand up under the scrutiny of Scripture! Let us think about good decision-making under the following three headings:

1. Happenings or hints?
2. Opening or closing doors?
3. Putting out a fleece?

## Happenings or hints?

People love to enshrine daily events by attaching religious significance to them. Instead of seeing them as mere 'happenings', they regard them as 'hints' from God. These events take on the status of 'revelation', encoded messages from God. After decoding these 'heavenly e-mails', people then base decisions upon them. This is very dangerous and highly subjective. Happenings are just happenings. They are not hints. It is completely inappropriate to ask: 'What is God telling me in this happening?' Once we go down that track we have departed from orthodox Christianity. We sail into an endless sea of subjectivism and ambiguity. Let us consider three practical examples.

*a. The burning church*

A growing congregation was deciding whether to expand its existing buildings, or knock them down and build bigger and better ones in their place, or sell-off the property and relocate elsewhere. But then something unexpected happened. A severe storm came, and lightning struck the church buildings setting them on fire. However, the Fire Brigade arrived quickly and saved the shell. It was quite amazing: the roof and walls were destroyed but the framework was essentially undamaged.

The next congregational meeting was very interesting. People were interpreting these 'happenings' as divine messages! One group said: 'The fact that the frame is undamaged is a miracle! God is telling us to rebuild and stay here.'

Others disagreed: 'There is no point patching up an old shell. God has shown us what to do with the old church by taking the first step and destroying most of it. We should take the hint and finish what he started. Knock it all down and build something better.'

A third section of the congregation said: 'The clear message is that our future is not here. The building has gone and that is God's way of telling us to go with it. Sell up and move from here!'

Then, as if that was not enough, a fourth group decoded the heavenly e-mail as follows: 'This is a judgement from God to warn us that he is displeased. There is some sin in our midst that is holding back our work. We are so preoccupied with buildings that we have neglected important spiritual matters. By destroying our buildings God has shown that he wants us to examine ourselves. We should forget about buildings and get serious about the Bible. We can meet in the school or hire the town hall!'

Do you see the problem? All these people have made the same mistake of enshrining daily events with religious significance. Instead of seeing them as mere 'happenings', they regard them as 'hints' from God. There are no rules here. It is completely subjective and full of ambiguity. It is sheer mysticism! One guess is as good as another. So be quite clear ... *happenings are not hints! They are just happenings*. There is always a mystery in providence.[1]

This calls for wisdom! Great care is needed when placing spiritual interpretations on historical events. We simply *do not* and *cannot* know why God sends a flood, a drought,

> We simply *do not* and *cannot* know why God sends a flood, a drought, a fire, or an earthquake. Unless the Bible tells us, the mystery remains ... we are not privy to the mind of God.

a fire, or an earthquake. Unless the Bible tells us, the mystery remains. Every opinion should be tentative rather than dogmatic. We know why Noah's flood happened because the Bible tells us. We know how to interpret the fire on Sodom and Gomorrah because Scripture is very clear. There is no ambiguity about the plagues in Egypt because the Bible explains them. But mostly we are not privy to the mind of God.

If we ignore this truth we are bound to hurt people needlessly. Christians in Australia have often been guilty of giving 'infallible' interpretations of providence. They do not hesitate to assert that droughts and bushfires are God's judgement on our sinful nation for moving further away from biblical standards. Why then are the farmers and country folk suffering most? Are they more sinful than people in the cities? Have people in the bush departed further from God than those in the 'red-light' districts of Sydney, where there are no droughts or bushfires?

*b. The falling tower*

One day some people told Jesus about two happenings: a deliberate mass-murder in Galilee, and the accidental death of eighteen people in Siloam where a tower collapsed on them. From our Lord's response it is clear that people were reading various 'messages' from these events. They not only read them as judgements from God, but as proof that the victims were more sinful than others. But Jesus dismissed such reasoning: 'Do you think that these Galileans were worse sinners than all the other Galileans because they suffered this way? I tell you, no! But unless you repent, you too will all perish. Or those eighteen who died when the tower in Siloam fell on them —

do you think they were more guilty than all the others living in Jerusalem? I tell you, no! But unless you repent, you too will all perish' (Luke 13:2-5). Jesus tells them that these events are simply happenings not hints! We have no right to baptize day-to-day events with the status of a divine message! God sends no e-mails!

## c. *The mystery of providence*

The key principle here is summarized in the Bible's Wisdom literature. 'As you do not know the path of the wind, or how the body is formed in a mother's womb, so you cannot understand the work of God, the Maker of all things. Sow your seed in the morning, and at evening, let not your hands be idle, for you do not know which will succeed, whether this or that, or whether both will do equally well' (Ecclesiastes 11:5-6).

In other words, stop pretending you can read God's mind out of daily events! *You cannot understand the activity of God!* It is very dangerous to read 'heavenly hints' into the happenings of life. Just get on with your duty … sow your seed in the morning. You cannot tell what God will do with your efforts. The crop may bear fruit or it may fail. 'You do not know which will succeed.' The mystery of daily providence remains a mystery. God sends no e-mails!

## Opening or closing doors?

Since the Bible does refer to some circumstances as 'doors' opened by God, we can legitimately talk about 'open doors' in our decision-making. But the real question is whether they indicate the will of God. If God opens a door, is that equivalent to divine leading? Is God beckoning us in? Is it a 'hint' of what he wants us to do? Is it compulsory for us to walk through an 'open door'?

The answer is 'No', as a careful study of the New Testament references will prove (Acts 14:27; 1 Corinthians 16:9; 2 Corinthians 2:12; Colossians 4:3; Revelation 3:8). An 'open door' is simply a God-given opportunity for enabling (facilitating) a desirable thing. When we read, 'God ... opened the door of faith to the Gentiles' (Acts 14:27) it means God created an opportunity for evangelizing the Gentiles. Paul and Barnabas made good use of it.

> God's open doors are gracious opportunities, but they are not imperatives ... that must be obeyed ... we are free to take them up or bypass them.

God's open doors are gracious opportunities, but they are not imperatives. They are not directions that must be obeyed. They graciously enlarge our potential, but we are free to take them up or bypass them. This is made obvious by comparing an open door entered by the apostle Paul and an open door that he bypassed.

*An open door entered*

At the end of his letter, Paul told the Corinthian church that he was looking forward to visiting them. 'I do not want to see you now and make only a passing visit; I hope to spend some time with you, if the Lord permits. But I will stay on at Ephesus until Pentecost, because a great door for effective work has opened to me, and there are many who oppose me' (1 Corinthians 16:7-9). He regarded the open door at Ephesus as a providential opportunity, not a sign from God. He wanted to stay there for the objective factual reason of much opposition. He could see that someone with the authority of an Apostle was needed in Ephesus to overcome hostility to the gospel. So he seized the opportunity to preach the gospel and resist the attacks.

## An open door bypassed

'Now when I went to Troas to preach the gospel of Christ and found that the Lord had opened a door for me, I still had no peace of mind, because I did not find my brother Titus there. So I said goodbye to them and went on to Macedonia' (2 Corinthians 2:12-13). Paul did not enter that open door! When he says, 'I still had no peace of mind', he is not talking about the need to 'feel a real peace about knowing God's will'. On the contrary, it refers to Paul's grave concerns for the state of the Corinthian church. He had written a severe letter to them (see 2 Corinthians 7:8), which was disciplinary in nature. Titus delivered the letter, and Paul planned to meet him in Troas for a first-hand report on how the Corinthians had reacted.

But Paul did not find Titus in Troas, so he left. He was well aware that the open door in Troas meant a real opportunity for church planting. But he walked away from it! He decided to go to Macedonia to find Titus. Why did Paul leave an open door, a door opened by God? If an 'open door' is a statement of God's will that believers must obey, then Paul's action is inexplicable, even sinful. If God sends e-mails, who are we to disobey? But if these things are seen correctly as gracious opportunities to be weighed up alongside all other options, then Paul's action is perfectly understandable and faithful. Rather than build a new house in Troas, Paul hurried to put out the flames threatening the house already built in Corinth.

So open doors are not revelations of God's will. It is not uncommon for Christians to be faced with several open doors at one time. A preacher can have several churches desiring to call him. He cannot possibly walk through all the doors. He is free to choose one or none of them![2]

It is worth noting that Scripture does not speak of 'closed doors'. If Paul was sovereignly prevented from pursuing a good and wise plan, he simply waited and tried again later. He did not interpret providential hindrances as 'no-go' (closed door) messages from God, as if God was saying, 'Your plan is faulty so forget it.' Several times he was prevented from going to Rome, but eventually he got there (Romans 15:22).

## Putting out a fleece?

Those who believe they need to 'put out a fleece' think along these lines: 'Lord, if you want me to carry out plan A, please let a particular event happen to indicate your will.' So the 'fleece' can be any event they choose: 'Please let the phone ring before 6.00pm', or 'Please let an old friend come to visit this weekend', or 'Let me hear a favourite hymn on the radio', or ... 'If the Brisbane Bullets beat the Perth Wildcats in the basketball playoffs that will be my sign!'

There are many serious problems here. It is based on a misunderstanding of Gideon's behaviour in Judges chapter 6. He should not have put God to the test.[3] It is also childish and random. Phones ring whether you have a decision to make or not! It is quite artificial to base a decision on the outcome of any random event. If a win by a designated basketball team is your guide to God's will, what if you asked for the opposite result? Will God co-operate with that request also? Will God change the whole course of sporting history just to drop a hint of guidance to an immature Christian? Will God even prevent the better team from winning just to satisfy an arbitrary request from someone who needs to grow up?

'Fleece' guidance is wide open to selfishness and presumption. What if two Christians ask for the opposite sign (rain today versus no rain today)? What if one sign-seeker wants the Brisbane Bullets to win while another wants the Perth Wildcats to win? What if there is no winner or loser because the match is cancelled or drawn? This is highly manipulative 'guidance'. Like a lot of political surveys, the result is largely decided by the terms stipulated.

Away with these pitiful, immature things! These giant corns need to be trodden on! We have all the guidance we need in the sixty-six books of the Bible. We have the whole counsel of God to equip the saints for 'every good work'. Nothing is to be added to it by revelations of the Spirit or the traditions of men! God sends no e-mails!

## Questions

1. *What principles are provided in Ephesians 5:15-21 for interpreting and responding to providence (daily events)?*

2. *Using James 1:5-7; Proverbs 2:1-4; and Colossians 1:9-10, how would you assess the following advice: 'Don't ask God for "hints" or "signs" — ask him for wisdom'?*

3. *'The key to guidance is a mind transformed by Scripture.' Is that a fair comment? See Psalm 119:9-16 and Romans 12:1-2.*

# 5. Decisions, decisions, decisions!

*Please read: Psalm 119:29-32*

We face decisions every day. Some are easy and some are hard. Some you can take plenty of time over, others are urgent. One of the beauties of a holiday is the respite from daily pressure, but there are still decisions to make. Will I go fishing today? Will I try the run-in tide or the run-out tide? We cannot escape decisions! But there are some snares to avoid. To make these dangers tangible, we will consider a fairly typical case.

A Christian man needs to buy a car ... let's call him Careful Colin. His search for a suitable vehicle is wide, diligent and thorough. As a result, Colin narrows his interest down to two cars (on opposite sides of town): a Ford Falcon at Strathpine (in the northern suburbs) and a Holden Commodore at Springwood (in the south). Both cars are in immaculate condition with good mechanical test results. Both cars suit his needs, and both are similarly priced. Which one will he buy? It is very hard to prefer one to the other. So Colin decided to take one more drive in each car.

After driving the Ford he was ready to buy it on the spot, and he came very close to doing so. But his mind kept thinking of that A-1 Commodore at Springwood! So he said to himself, 'I'll go to Springwood and drive the Holden again ... then I'll come back here and if God wants me to have the Ford Falcon, it will still be here when I return. If not, it obviously wasn't God's will for me, and I'll settle for the Commodore.' Having done all that, he remained happy with both cars, and when he returned to Strathpine the Falcon was still there. His heart leaped for joy. Colin took this as a sign of confirmation from God, so he drove away in his new car, relieved that the decision was over.

We see a strange mixture of wisdom and folly here, and it recurs with lots of Christians in lots of decisions. Careful Colin could be any one of us. Whether the issue is buying a car or a house or a family dog, or selecting subjects for next year at school or university, there are traps to avoid. Colin's case highlights some of them, namely:

1. Beware of fantasy
2. Beware of guilt trips
3. Beware of subjectivism

## Beware of fantasy

Fantasy involves playing 'mind games' ... imagining what you would like to believe and then acting as if it was *true* rather than mere fantasy! In Colin's case his fantasy is another form of 'putting out a fleece'. He arranges a little test in his mind by which he can force God to show his hand. In this mind game Colin assumes he can see into the secret will of God, discovering what God would otherwise have kept secret. And when the 'rules' of Colin's little fantasy produce a result (namely, the Ford Falcon is still for sale two hours later), he believes the whole fantasy is not fantasy at all!

Colin thinks it is sober, objective reality! He actually believes that God really is telling him what he wants Colin to do! Tragically he has no doubt that God is playing by the rules of a silly little game invented by Colin! His fantasy was bad enough, seeking to force God's secret will out into the public domain. But now it is worse. Colin is deluded into thinking that all this is true!

But it is sheer nonsense! For a start it is a complete misunderstanding of the sovereign (secret) will of God! All the way along Colin was absolutely free to buy the Falcon! Whether he purchased it or not, the sovereign will of God was done. God's sovereign will cannot be known until after the event. It permits plenty of things that he does not approve! It includes things for which God will eventually judge us, things that he rules and overrules as he sees fit. Even if Colin had stolen the car or vandalized it, this would all occur within the sovereign (secret) will of God. Not even Satan can act contrary to the secret will of God! Even if we knew the details, God's secret will is no use in our decision-making. The revealed will of God is all we have and all we need. It says Colin is not to steal or harm his neighbour's property. It also says Colin is free to buy any car he chooses. That is all Colin needs to know.

Away with the fantasy! In this car-buying exercise the reality is simple. As long as the car is legally for sale, Colin is perfectly free to buy the Ford or not buy it! Any other customer is likewise free. The question is not whether *God* wants you to buy it. The question is, 'Do *you* want to buy it?' So long as all biblical principles are observed the ball is in Colin's court. God is not going to tell him any more! God sends no e-mails! God will not make the decision for Colin! Colin is (supposedly) a big boy now!

*A practical lesson*

Be realistic in decisions about careers. People fantasize by 'seeing themselves in their mind's eye' as a doctor, lawyer, teacher, mother ... whatever. Inevitably the attractions and desirable aspects of each career drive the fantasy. They dream of 'how good it will be', but the reality is different. There is a difficult, negative, unglamorous and unpalatable side to every career path. The Adamic curse hits everyone. 'Cursed is the ground because of you; through painful toil you will eat of it all the days of your life. It will produce thorns and thistles for you... By the sweat of your brow you will eat your food' (Genesis 3:17-19).

> **Don't make decisions on the basis of fantasy! Be realistic! Face up to the downside! Don't look at things 'romantically', 'wistfully', or 'idealistically'.**

We must be alert to the 'grass is greener' mentality. It is sheer fantasy! Every car you buy will have negatives as well as (hopefully) some positives. The same goes for every house, every career, and every marriage partner. Don't make decisions on the basis of fantasy! Be realistic! Face up to the downside! Don't look at things 'romantically', 'wistfully', or 'idealistically'.

## Beware of guilt trips

Hindsight is a great problem. We all know more after a decision than before it. We all see more clearly after the event. This is just another way of saying you can't know the secret will of God until it happens. This hindsight is a real trap for the unwary. It leads many people on a guilt trip. They torture themselves, wishing they'd decided differently. The road to a guilt trip begins at the gate marked 'if only'. If only I'd done this ... if only I'd seen that! If only I'd followed the technician's advice rather than the salesman's pitch!

Think about Careful Colin again. We saw him driving off happily into the sunset in his A-1, pre-loved, one careful owner, low mileage Ford Falcon, comforted by all the reassuring sales talk ... *'first to see will buy, immaculate, reluctant sale, always garaged, owner going overseas'*. Next day he proudly shows off his car at a family picnic, but is embarrassed by a flat battery. It costs him $100 (£45) for the battery and $250 for a mechanic to fix the damage to the engine's computer system caused by Colin trying to jump-start it incorrectly. But Colin coped fairly well, reassuring himself that even the best cars get flat batteries.

Then a list of car problems beset him over the ensuing months. The scrubbing front tyres required the fitting of a camber kit worth $400. Then the thermostat failed, causing the engine to overheat. Repairs to the warped cylinder head cost him $900 but, as he was told, he should be glad it wasn't an eight-cylinder motor. That would have cost him twice as much. Then a stone went through the windscreen. It was covered by insurance but Colin had to pay the first $200 as 'excess'. Repairs to the car cost him $1,850 in the first month!

Just one day after Colin had the new glass fitted, a furniture truck ran into the back of him in peak-hour traffic. Poor old Colin was three weeks without his car, and when he got it back from the panel shop it was never the same again. He was unhappy with the repairs, and it now leaked when he washed it. But the next two months were trouble free and Colin thought the worst was over. Then, just two days after the warranty expired, a terrible noise came out of the automatic transmission as it grated to a stop. It had to be completely rebuilt, and since modern electronically modulated gearboxes are very costly, Colin was another $2700 out of pocket!

What is Colin saying to himself now? 'If only … if only … if only!' He's on a guilt trip. He tortures himself: 'If only I'd chosen the Commodore! … If only I'd done more homework ... if only I'd purchased new, not second-hand! ... If only I'd kept the old car, it was so reliable! ... I nearly decided to spend the money on house extensions rather than the car ... if only I'd done so! … If only I knew then what I know now.' We can all become agitated like this, but for several reasons it is very foolish.

Firstly, you cannot go back. You can never turn 'hindsight' into 'foresight'. Even if different decisions may have produced happier results, you cannot turn the clock back to actually make those different decisions, so why torment yourself?

Secondly, you cannot predict how the alternative choices would have turned out. Suppose Colin had bought the Commodore. Do those cars never break down? Suppose he kept the old car. Don't old cars break down? Suppose he bought a brand new car. Are new cars perfectly trouble-free? If he spent the money on house extensions, would that have been without difficulties? Colin actually has friends who are carrying out house renovations and extensions. Do they face problems? Is renovation free of hidden extras, council inspectors, breakdowns, delays and frustrations? Perhaps they are so stressed that they wish they'd left the house alone and bought Colin's car! The grass is always greener...!

Thirdly, once you start a guilt trip, where do you stop? The 'if only' road never ends. Every one of us could improve on every single thing we have ever done 'if only' certain things applied. If only I was good at maths ... if only I was athletic ... if only my parents had more money ... if only I'd been able to complete my education ... if only I hadn't been sick at the time. This whole agenda is sin! Let's get that clear! It is a sinful, faithless, denial of God's providence. God does not expect us to be all-knowing, infallible and inerrant. He alone has those abilities. The Lord knows we are frail children of dust. He expects us to do what is right and responsible and reasonable for humans to do — but no more! God expects us to trust him for the outworking of all things, even when good decisions bring unpleasant and totally unexpected results!

Of course, if hindsight reveals that we did act in a foolish, hasty way — if we were unwise or should have known better, if we were too headstrong or prejudiced to listen — we should repent and learn a good lesson. And then *get over it!* Don't

> Be careful not to enshrine 'happenings' as messages from God. It is a snare that many fall into.

dwell on past mistakes. Leave it in the past and get on with your life, trusting God to do what he does for all his people, causing even our mistakes to work together with all other things for our good.

Hindsight is a dangerous and fallible judge at the best of times. Even when the results of a decision turn out as you had hoped, you should not interpret this as God confirming and approving your decision.[1] A student might do well at his studies. God blesses him with good results. But this should not be interpreted as confirmation of the will of God for his career. A person with academic gifts would also get good results in many other courses. Be careful not to enshrine 'happenings' as messages from God. It is a snare that many fall into.

*What if things go wrong?*

When things go 'wrong' after you make a decision ... when hardships and unexpected problems arise as a direct result ... we cannot automatically assume this is God telling us to turn back. It is not God's way of saying it was a bad decision that you should not have made. Jesus made the right decision in the Garden of Gethsemane, but look where it led him! Look at that bitter cup he drank at Golgotha! Look where Daniel's stand against idolatry led him — into the lion's den! Look what Job's unblemished character got him: satanic assault. Look where Jeremiah's good preaching got him! Look at the abuse Amos suffered for being an obedient prophet. The martyrs burned at the stake for their good decisions. Beware of guilt trips arising from hindsight.

## Beware of subjectivism

There is of course a subjective side to life. We all have feelings, yearnings, preferences, tastes, emotions and hunches. The Bible recognizes these things. God has made us as very complex psychosomatic beings. Often how we 'feel' about something cannot be understood or analysed even by us. We might not know *why* we feel like we do ... we just do! The next chapter will focus on this matter, but for now I simply urge you not to interpret 'feelings' as 'the leading of the Spirit'.

Like everything else, feelings must be assessed and judged by the plain teachings of the Bible. It is dangerous to attribute your feelings to the Holy Spirit. How do you know where your feelings come from? Why do you feel inclined to some colours and disinclined to others? And why does it differ from person to person? How can you trace the mysterious movements of your own human spirit, let alone the infinite Holy Spirit? Where do your feelings and hunches and premonitions come from? Was it due to an active imagination, a disturbing book, an amazing experience, a side effect of medication, or stress?

Feelings have a proper function, but it is not to determine the will of God! This does not mean we should ignore or suppress our feelings. But we must keep them within biblical parameters. Two questions are in order: *Why be a mystic?* and *Why be a martyr?*

## 1. *Why be a mystic?* (The mystic complex)

Mystics put pious-religious interpretations on feelings. They can be heard saying, 'I felt led to do this.' The impression given is that God has been dropping little hints, prodding and suggesting the way to go. Mystics act as though they are acutely sensitive to these divine hints. They talk about being 'open to the leading of the Lord'. Their religious antennae pick up spiritual vibes that the rest of us apparently miss.

In fact all of us should simply say 'I preferred' or 'I decided'. Don't interpret how you feel as the leading of God: just be honest and say it is how you feel! As long as those feelings are appropriate they can help shape your decisions. We can see an illustration by returning to Careful Colin. He found two good cars admirably suiting his needs, but for various reasons he likes one more than the other. He 'feels' more inclined to the Ford than the Holden. It might be because of the colour, the shape, or the throaty sound of the exhaust. Perhaps it brings back happy memories of the old family Ford car his Mum and Dad owned. Maybe Colin himself doesn't know why he feels inclined to one rather than the other, but he does. That's okay! God is happy for us to have those subjective feelings. They are morally neutral.

Colin should buy the car he likes best! But in doing so he should not attribute his inner hunches and feelings to God! He should not read them mystically as divine instruction, the leading of God. It is all Colin, and Colin is free to like a white car more than a red car, and he is free to prefer the throaty roar of a V-8 rather than the frantic sound of a high revving 4-cylinder car. He is free to simply *like* one car more than the other for inexplicable reasons — but when he follows his feelings, let him be honest. Let him say, 'I like this better, I prefer this one, I decided this way.' Away with the mystical 'I felt God leading me.'

*2. Why be a martyr?* (The martyr complex)

Subjectivity can work in reverse. For example, a Christian is ready to serve overseas, and the mission society has two vacancies to fill. One is in Europe where living standards are good; the other is in a poor nation with appalling health standards, ravaged by civil war. Which one will the dedicated missionary go to, assuming he has the skills needed in both places?

He is often pressured by a mixture of guilt and pride to take the most unpleasant role, to make the greatest sacrifice, and to interpret the greatest need as 'God's will'. This reverse form of 'subjective guidance' says: 'It's not going to look very spiritual if I choose the vacancy I prefer. It is more spiritual to do something you dislike, making a greater sacrifice. So I'll take the poverty option.'

Such people actually feel guilty choosing blessed things! The problem here is the denial of true freedom, including the freedom to choose an altogether different career at home. It is also an unwitting smear upon the character of God, as if he is a hard taskmaster who wants us to choose unpleasant options. The truth is, 'God … richly provides us with everything for our enjoyment' (1 Timothy 6:17). 'Man's chief end is to glorify God and enjoy him for ever' (*Westminster Shorter Catechism*, question 1).

Decisions, decisions, decisions! Beware of the traps — fantasy, guilt tripping and subjectivism. May God grant us all greater and greater maturity.

## Questions

1. *Even before making decisions, certain fundamental truths should be recognized. What are they? (See Psalm 33:11; Proverbs 19:21; & Isaiah 14:27; 46:9-10.)*

2. *Good and faithful decisions can lead to trouble. How does Hebrews 11:32-39 equip us in such cases?*

3. *To what extent does immaturity cause decision-making problems? (See Hebrews 5:11-14.)*

# 6. O what a feeling!

*Please read: 1 Corinthians 2*

The word 'Toyota' indicates good cars, but not good theology. 'O what a feeling!' is the current message of their advertising campaign that echoes across the market. In other words, their cars feel good and good feelings mean good vehicles, so buy them! Be guided by your feelings! Unfortunately, that philosophy also defines the theology of many Christians. What they 'buy into' is based on how it feels.

To some extent our feelings are involved in every choice we make. But in the end they must be held in check by objective facts. You might feel inclined to buy a car because it feels very smooth and quiet and safe. But a wise man knows that not all that glitters is gold. An expert who will be guided by facts not feelings should examine the car. Very dangerous things can feel good. Alternatively, a car might feel terrible to you, yet in reality be a very good vehicle.

When we look around the Christian community today, there is a lot of 'Toyota theology': ways of living and speaking based on feelings. The objective facts of divine revelation are unwittingly pushed aside. The Bible is not openly denied. It is still consulted and believed, but a sea of subjectivism swamps it. In addressing this matter of feelings, three issues in our culture need urgent scrutiny:

1. Religious confusion
2. 'Peace with God'?
3. Religious blackmail


## Religious confusion

Among God's people there is a widespread confusion lying at the heart of Christian guidance. It is caused by a failure to distinguish two very important works of the Holy Spirit. We can describe these two vital ministries as the Holy Spirit giving us his mind, and the Holy Spirit giving us himself.

### The Holy Spirit giving us his mind

As we saw in chapter two, this is God's 'upfront' guidance, where he tells us his will. The Bible is the word of the Holy Spirit: 'All Scripture is God-spirited' (God-breathed, 2 Timothy 3:16). The Bible is where God 'talks' to us, telling us what he wants. The Bible is where God the Holy Spirit reveals his mind: 'Men spoke from God as they were carried along by the Holy Spirit' (2 Peter 1:21).

Concerning the original writers, this ministry of the Holy Spirit is called *inspiration*. The Holy Spirit supervised and overshadowed the whole process of writing so that the human authors were preserved from error. But with regard to us as readers of the Word, this ministry of the Holy Spirit is called *illumination*. The Lord enlightens our minds so that we can understand what is written. 'The man without the Spirit does not accept the things that come from the Spirit of God, for they are foolishness to him, and he cannot understand them, because they are spiritually discerned' (1 Corinthians 2:14). So we rightly confess that the whole Bible (all sixty-six books) is a full, sufficient and comprehensive statement of the will of God. It tells us all we need to know in order to please God in all the decisions we make. This 'whole counsel of God' is so complete that 'Nothing at any time is to be added, whether by new revelations of the Spirit, or human traditions' (*Westminster Confession*, 1:6).

*The Holy Spirit giving himself*

This is the wonderful work of the Spirit as our *comforter*. Jesus calls him the 'Paraclete' (counsellor, helper, or comforter). 'And I will ask the Father, and he will give you another Counsellor to be with you for ever — the Spirit of truth. The world cannot accept him, because it neither sees him nor knows him. But you know him, for he lives with you and will be in you' (John 14:16-17). He comes in person to us at various times, and in various ways, providing help for God's children according to our different needs and circumstances.

He comes to help, to warn, to protect, to strengthen, to motivate, to revive, or to encourage. In other words, we come to experience *God himself.* This is not the Spirit revealing his will and word. That has ceased with the Bible. Rather, this is the Spirit revealing himself. This is God drawing close to us in his gracious embrace. The distinction between these two ministries of the Holy Spirit is the distinction between *Christian guidance* and *Christian experience.*

The guidance is *uniform and normative* because the same Bible tells all of us the same revealed will of God. All of us must live by the same inspired words. Within that uniform framework we are free to make personal decisions. But the Christian experience is *multiform and non-normative.* It is different for every Christian. No Christian can expect or require anyone else to have all the same spiritual experiences.

Only Moses had a 'burning bush experience', no one else. Only Jacob wrestled with God, no one else. Only Peter, James and John experienced the transfiguration of Jesus, no one else. Only 120 believers had the Pentecost experience. It is simply impossible for anyone else to be in the same situation. Only *I* can have my particular experiences of the Lord's personal dealings. They are very dear and very real. But it is wrong to interpret them as God telling me something. Indeed, my personal experiences of God must be interpreted by what God tells everyone else, his written word, the Bible.

We must stop confusing the Holy Spirit's ministry as the Comforter with his ministry as the teacher and revealer of truth. They are both very real and vital but they are not the same. You cannot equate experience and guidance! You cannot say that what you feel is what God has said! You must be very careful not to put infallible interpretations upon your spiritual experiences. There is always a degree of mystery in experience (providence).

*Experiences have boundaries*

It is a wonderful thing to experience God's everlasting arms in a vivid and heightened way. But he is guarding us whether we feel it or not! Sometimes God graciously lets us feel his presence in special seasons. Rejoice in it, yes! Praise God for it, yes! But be wary of how you understand any experience. Scripture alone is the inspired judge. And be careful what you tell others. They should not be left feeling inferior or searching for a similar experience.

Like all subjective things, beauty is in the eye of the beholder. That is why subjective guidance is dangerous. Two people can have completely opposite feelings about the same thing. For example, consider the decision to buy a car. Car 'A' feels good. It is whisper-quiet with a silky smooth gearbox. It floats over bumps, and you say (approvingly), 'O what a feeling!' But car 'B' is quite different. It feels bad and you dislike it. After driving it you say, 'O what a feeling' (disapprovingly). But that may reveal more about you than the car. Your feelings about the car may be due to ignorance of mechanical things!

> It is a wonderful thing to experience God's everlasting arms in a vivid and heightened way. But he is guarding us whether we feel it or not!

Then along comes Michael Schumacher, the champion race-car driver. He also notices that car 'B' will not idle smoothly and it has a sudden clutch. He too notices a harsh suspension that accentuates every bump. He feels the tight gearbox with its short robust shift pattern. He senses that this car runs and smells very hot, and has a noisy growl to it. But his eyes light up. He knows what lies behind all those feelings.

He knows it idles roughly because of the advanced camshaft and high compression cylinder heads. It only becomes smooth at 5000rpm when the turbocharger kicks in. He knows it doesn't cushion bumps like a Citroen because it has track-tuned suspension and ultra low profile tyres. It is a lot noisier than a limousine because extractors and a straight-through exhaust system scavenge the high-performance engine. The gearbox is quite stiff because it is identical to those used in Army troop carriers. It will outlast Methuselah. In summary, it is a very high quality car, far safer and stronger than traditional family cars. It is technically superior to most other vehicles on the road. So Michael Schumacher says, 'O what a feeling' and buys it! Beauty is in the eye of the beholder! One man's meat is another man's poison!

What you feel is what you feel — no more and no less. You must not 'baptize' your feelings with divine sanction. Don't say this feeling is from God! Don't expect it to be typical or normal or right for anyone else just because it is for you. I can't imagine many women being attracted to Car 'B' (even after Michael Schumacher explained how good those unpleasant feelings really were). But a good number of men would be tempted. Hopefully the point is made. We must stop the confusion. A feeling is just a feeling, and nothing more. A hunch is merely a hunch. An idea or a dream or a vision (or whatever name you give to your experience) can be nothing more than a subjective experience. Such things can be useful, but they are not revelations of God's will.

*Here is proof!*

We see proof in 1 Timothy 3:1, where a strong desire and yearning for the task of oversight in the church is good: 'Here is a trustworthy saying: If anyone sets his heart on being an overseer, he desires a noble task.' But that's all it is, a valid desire, a legitimate feeling. Paul immediately makes it clear that unless a man has the objective qualifications, the feeling is no guide at all. He must be suitably gifted for the task. And even if he has both the desire and qualifications, it is still not mandatory that he be an overseer. He is still free to decline and serve God in other ways. Feelings do not amount to guidance.

## 'Peace with God'?

Many Christians create unnecessary problems for themselves about 'peace with God'. They think of it as a subjective concept, how we feel about God, or how we feel before God. That is why they bring it into matters of guidance and decision-making. They assume that godly decisions are accompanied by a sense of peace with God. But that does not accord with the New Testament data.

'Peace with God' is an objective term describing the judicial status of every true believer. It has nothing to do with our fickle feelings. Regardless of how we feel about anything, true believers always have 'peace with God'. We always have the status of being God's justified, reconciled and beloved people. 'Peace with God' is not something that comes and goes. It is not a 'feeling' of any sort, and it has nothing to do with making decisions (wisely or otherwise). To have 'peace with God' means being free of condemnation. It is the opposite of having 'enmity with God'. That is the universal reality for every non-Christian. But their 'enmity with God' is not something they feel. If only they did! Then they might be urgent to seek forgiveness. But it isn't a subjective quality. It is an objective quality describing their hostile status before God.

Likewise, 'peace with God' is a universal reality for every Christian. It is classically expressed by the apostle Paul: 'Therefore, since we have been justified through faith, we have peace with God through our Lord Jesus Christ' (Romans 5:1). The meaning is accurately captured by John Murray: '"Peace with God" denotes relationship with God. It is not the composure and tranquillity of our minds and hearts; it is the status of peace flowing from the reconciliation (vss.10, 11) and reflects primarily upon God's alienation from us and our instatement in his favour.'

> To have 'peace with God' means being free of condemnation ... That is a universal reality for every Christian.

It is true that this blessed relationship of peace with God will affect how we feel as we consciously reflect on it. But we must not confuse the two, so Murray immediately adds: 'Peace of heart and mind proceeds from "peace with God" and is the reflection in our consciousness of the relation established by justification. But it is the objective relation that is in view here when Paul speaks of "peace with God".[1]

An illustration will assist us to make the proper distinctions. Despite his faults, Jonah was a true believer. As a prophet of God his attitude was far from commendable. Jonah did not want to preach to Gentiles in case they believed his sermons and found God's mercy. When he was finally forced to preach at Nineveh for forty days, he chose a 'ringside seat' hoping to see God destroy them. He could not hide his annoyance when God relented.

Paradoxically this twisted man was one of the most successful preachers in the Old Testament! One hundred and fifty thousand people responded properly to his 'doomsday' sermons. Throughout these events Jonah was a true believer. Redemptively his objective status was one of 'peace with God', yet his subjective condition was anything but peaceful. He was an agitated man.

How he managed to sleep below decks when a storm was swamping the ship is difficult to fathom. It certainly was not the sleep of a peaceful conscience. On the contrary, even before the lot fell on him, Jonah had told the pagan sailors he was running away from God (Jonah 1:10). His conscience accused him and he made them hurl him overboard to calm the storm. Even when Jonah was finally obeying God by preaching in Nineveh, he could not enjoy the fruits of a clear conscience. He preached under duress with bad attitudes, recently regurgitated from three days in the belly of a fish. So a feeling of peace with God does not automatically accompany all who have that objective status. Many other factors come into play (like faithfulness, motivation, gratitude and selflessness).

## Religious blackmail

Feelings can be wielded as weapons of emotional and spiritual blackmail. Whether this is deliberate or not is beside the point. It happens and it is wrong. Consider some examples. Beginning with 'The Lord laid it on my heart,' someone announces an opinion that allegedly comes from God. I have often witnessed this sort of thing in church committees and courts (such as a presbytery or assembly). Someone attributes his personal feelings to the Holy Spirit. To say 'The Lord has laid it on my heart' is both unproved and unprovable! It needs to be exposed as the sheer mysticism it is. Paradoxically, though it is often paraded as a humble and deeply spiritual form of Christianity, it is exceptionally arrogant and haughty, even when that is not intended.

It is arrogant because it demands an audience. It demands that everyone must listen and acquiesce because it (allegedly) comes from God. God has moved this person! God laid this message on his heart. God put him under constraint to tell you. Therefore woe betide you if you fail to sit up and listen obediently! This is cultic! That person implicitly claims the same authority as the inspired prophets and apostles! It is rampant throughout Christendom and across denominations! It can be readily exposed with the two following acid tests.

# O what a feeling!

Next time someone takes the holy ground, confronting you with 'The Lord laid something on my heart ... The Lord gave me this text ... God wants me to tell you', try this. As soon as you hear that introductory formula, just say: 'No — I'm not interested. Please don't say any more.' What do you think will happen?

You will be judged as very unspiritual. Your refusal to hear that person will be taken as a refusal to hear God, virtual blasphemy. And the speaker will feel his imaginary importance has been slighted. Indeed, you have brought him down a peg or two. It is now obvious that this entire mode of speech is a form of emotional and spiritual blackmail (even if not intended). Instead of two equal persons sitting down on equal terms to discuss an idea, there is class distinction. The passive needy person is expected to sit with baited breath, waiting for the pearls of inspired wisdom coming through God's hand-picked messenger! And when he announces the heavenly oracle, there is to be no debate. You should obey at once.

The simple fact is that 'The Lord laid it on my heart' is a pompous version of 'I have something I'd like to say.' The formula 'In my quiet-time this morning the Lord gave me this text' is a super-spiritual way of saying, 'A certain Bible truth really struck home: can I tell you about it?' And when someone says, 'The Lord placed this burden upon me', it is a pious way of saying, 'I'm quite concerned'. Let us stop playing prophets and priests! Let us stop the pious blackmail and cease from attributing our feelings to God the Holy Spirit. That is the real blasphemy! That is putting words in God's mouth — words he did not speak!

*Acid test 2*

When you are in a meeting debating a contentious matter, someone may say: 'I move the following motion which the Lord has laid on my heart ... it comes straight out of the text he so vividly gave me in my quiet time this morning ... the Lord has placed a real burden on me about the decision we should make, so I move that we...'

Suppose it was true! Who could ever oppose or amend that motion? It has the support of God! It allegedly comes from Scripture and the Holy Spirit. A person on earth is moving a motion written in heaven! Who could dare debate it or question it? This is Toyota theology: O what a feeling!

If a person has strong feelings, strong subjective desires, they should honestly say, 'My strong personal feeling is...' Then others could freely differ, expressing their strong feelings in the opposite direction. This would lead to a rational debate in an objective factual manner. Instead, a haughty religious note has been sounded. A high and mighty posture has been taken. What is being held over that meeting is not merely one man's feelings, which are challengeable and fallible, but the feelings of God the Holy Spirit, which are unchallengeable and infallible! And if someone with a better grasp of theology is present, and he disagrees with the speaker for 'baptizing' his feelings, a very unpleasant scene inevitably follows. Whoever challenges this plague of mysticism risks being branded as arrogant, unspiritual and unloving. In fact the real arrogance is on the other side.

You are free to have a Toyota car but you are not free to have a Toyota theology. Feelings are inevitable, normal and sometimes intensely spiritual, but they are still only feelings. They are naturally involved in decision-making but they must be held in check. *Feelings must not become oracles.* They must yield to the objective truth of Scripture. That alone is the voice of God guiding us! May God help us to avoid both religious confusion and religious blackmail!

## Questions

1. *'Eliphaz's appeal to feelings and visions in his misguided debate with Job is a sober warning for us all.' Assess that in the light of Job 4:12-19 and 42:7-9.*

2. *Regardless of a man's strong subjective feelings, what are the objective qualities required of him before he can become a leader in the church? (See 1 Timothy 3:1-13.)*

3. *Why is a person's religious/spiritual experience not a trustworthy guide? (See 1 Timothy 4:1-8 and 2 Thessalonians 2:9-16.)*

# 7. What about Scripture?

*Please read: 2 Timothy 3*

The doctrine of Scripture has fallen on hard times. In practice, many churchgoers have lost confidence in their Bibles. They accept it as the Word of God, and they accept that it answers fundamental questions about sin and salvation, but they do not see its relevance for the many issues of daily life. Subjective forms of guidance are therefore common.

Seemingly unaware of church history Christians today are repeating ancient mistakes. Mystical talk about 'feeling led' is nothing new, nor is the habit of 'baptizing' various experiences as the promptings of God. These problems are well documented in the history of groups like the Montanists, Pietists and Quakers. If we ignore the lessons of the past we are bound to repeat its errors, and that is happening today. The proper way to stem this tide is to promote the doctrine of Scripture in all its richness. That will equip people to use the

Bible properly themselves and help others out of the morass of mysticism.

In summary we need to return to the doctrine of Scripture embraced by orthodox historic Protestant Christianity. Since the first chapter of the *Westminster Confession of Faith* states it well, that will serve as a good focal point. Other great creeds of Christianity teach the same fundamental truths. Consider the first paragraph:

> Although the light of nature, and the works of creation and providence so clearly reveal the goodness, wisdom, and power of God, that humans are without excuse, yet they are not sufficient to give that knowledge of God and of His will which is necessary for salvation. Therefore it pleased the Lord, at different times, and in various ways, to reveal Himself, and to declare His will to His church. Afterwards, for the better preserving and spreading of the truth, and for the more sure establishment and comfort of the church against the corruption of the flesh, and the malice of Satan and of the world, God caused this revelation of Himself and His will to be put in writing. This writing, the Holy Scripture, is therefore essential because God's former ways of revealing His will to His people have ceased.

Four times Scripture is called God's 'will'. To know God's will means to know Scripture, not some private 'will of God for my life'. As long as we act within biblical boundaries we are acting according to the will of God! Three great truths about Scripture are stressed here:

1. It is unique
2. It is in hard copy
3. It is finished

## Scripture is unique

There are other forms of divine revelation apart from Scripture. They are all significant, and they all have a role to play, but Scripture is unique because it alone shows God's plan of salvation. It is common to distinguish between 'general revelation' and 'special revelation'.

*General revelation*

That is what the *Westminster Confession* means by 'the light of nature, and the works of creation and providence'. As men look out at the world and upwards to the sun, moon and stars, and as they observe complexity in the biggest things (outer space) and the tiniest things (atoms and cells), they are seeing God's creative genius displayed. This revelation holds men fully accountable to God. It 'so clearly reveals the goodness, wisdom, and power of God, that humans are without excuse'.

The Bible puts it this way: 'Since the creation of the world God's invisible qualities — his eternal power and divine nature — have been clearly seen, being understood from what has been made, so that men are without excuse' (Romans 1:20).

The 'light of nature' includes man's intelligence and powers of logical reasoning. This is what Paul appealed to in Athens when he told the Greeks that their religion contradicted their own logic (Acts 17). Why did they leave gifts of food for their numerous icons, statues and idols when it was obvious that the God who made the world needs nothing? God's 'works of providence' include all the circumstances of daily life, such as rain, sunshine, family and his acts of judgement. This revelation also holds men fully accountable to God. Thus Pharaoh was expected to make some logical deductions from the ten plagues God sent upon Egypt! The King of Babylon was expected to make logical deductions from Daniel's unexpected safety in the lions' den and from God's providential care of Shadrach, Meshach and Abednego in the fiery furnace. Such providential circumstances reveal something about God!

> Humans can and do make all sorts of proper deductions from observing the sun, moon, stars and atoms. But such observations will never reveal what God requires if sinners are to be saved.

Whatever form it takes, 'general revelation' is sufficient to reveal God, forcing men to conclude that God's nature is eternally powerful, infinite and unique. It is enough to make man see that he should love God and live by the moral law of God written in his heart and conscience (Romans 2:14-15). Therefore 'general revelation' leaves man condemned and 'without excuse'.

Remember, from 'natural revelation' comes 'natural theology' (all the logical deductions implied by the creation). But both are inadequate. Humans can and do make all sorts of proper deductions from observing the sun, moon, stars and atoms. But such observations will never reveal what

God requires if sinners are to be saved. They cannot even show if a plan of salvation exists. 'Nature' is a limited tutor.

*Special revelation*

Since general revelation is 'not sufficient to give that knowledge of God and of His will, which is necessary for salvation', God graciously gave another (special) revelation that does show the way of salvation. 'Therefore it pleased the Lord, at different times, and in various ways, to reveal Himself, and to declare His will to His church.' This process went from the time of Moses (around 1500 B.C.) to the time of the last Apostle, John (around A.D. 90). God kept giving more and more detail of his saving plan, using various methods to convey his will.

Sometimes he made a personal appearance (a theophany). God spoke to Moses in the burning bush, to Job in the storm, and again with Moses at the cleft of a rock. At other times God spoke through angels, or dreams and visions. The Spirit of God also moved directly upon the hearts and minds of chosen instruments (prophets and apostles), revealing the divine will from heaven.

This historical process was always moving towards an end point, the final, unrepeatable, climax of special revelation. That arrived with God's Son, Jesus Christ. 'In the past God spoke to our forefathers through the prophets at many times and in various ways, but in these last days he has spoken to us by his Son' (Hebrews 1:1-2). Scripture is therefore unique revelation because it is redemptive. It sets out God's way of salvation and shows men what is required of them in order to be saved from the Adamic curse.

## Scripture is in hard copy

A hard copy is one that is written down in black and white: 'Afterwards, for the better preserving and spreading of the truth, and for the more sure establishment and comfort of the church against the corruption of the flesh, and the malice of Satan and of the world, God caused this revelation of Himself and His will to be put in writing.' This is very important.

The will of God is not up for grabs. It is not something inward, subjective, or intangible. It has nothing to do with our feelings. It is not something private or tailor-made for you or I alone. It is not a voice of revelation that you sense inside yourself. No, it is in hard copy! It is visible and written down. It is there in the arrangement of verbs and nouns, subjects and predicates, phrases and clauses, questions and exclamations, warnings and encouragements, parables and narratives, proverbs and psalms, history and typology, jots and tittles, prepositions and pronouns!

It is the most *public* property on earth. The Word of God is the very opposite of any private opinion. It has nothing to do with 'a wee small voice inside of me'. It is *public domain*. Everybody else has the very same Word of God. Everybody else can criticize your misuse of it or commend your proper use of it. It is open to radical scrutiny. Nothing on earth has been more scrutinized than the Bible.

Jesus repeatedly appealed to this visible objective feature of Scripture. 'It is written … again it is written'; 'Have you not read?'; 'Do not think I come to abolish the Law or the Prophets: until heaven and earth pass away, not the smallest letter or the least stroke of a pen, will by any means disappear.' This is hard-copy language. The will of God is a definite, tangible, recognizable, printed product. It is a known entity with measurements! We are responsible to treat it accordingly. The primary author (God) is not at variance with the secondary authors (human writers). God's revealed will is entirely harmonious, and no part can be interpreted in conflict with another part. And since it is literature, the proper rules of grammar, genre and context must be used to interpret it.

## Scripture is finished

'This writing, the Holy Scripture, is therefore essential because God's former ways of revealing His will to His people have ceased.' It needs to be stressed that it is not only Scripture that has finished. *Special revelation in its entirety has finished.* There is no more 'will of God' to be revealed. There are no other truths that Christians will need to receive, and guard, and obey, and teach to the world.

The Westminster delegates could hardly have stated it more plainly. Scripture is essential because 'God's former ways of revealing His will have ceased.' This confesses far more than a closed canon of sixty-six biblical books. There is no further revelatory *product* and no further revelatory *process*. God has ceased communicating his will. Even the old methods of revealing God's will have ceased: 'God's former ways of revealing His will to His people have ceased.'

That means God is not speaking any more through visions, dreams, theophanies, divine appearances, or angels! There are no more prophets or apostles. God finished speaking when he sent his Son. Everything Jesus had to say to his church was put into print in the twenty-seven books of the New Testament, and there it ends. Never again do private individuals get direct revelations from God (either to pass on to the church or just to keep for themselves).

Yes, this is a very big claim but it is absolutely basic to healthy Christianity. Some people oppose it by saying, 'You're limiting God.' On the basis of Christ's words in John 16:13, it is often claimed that the Holy Spirit is still leading us into 'all the truth'. But that is inconsistent with what Scripture teaches elsewhere. The context needs to be considered more carefully. It is certainly a promise from Jesus that is very relevant to the topic of guidance. But what does it mean? Our Lord said, 'When He, the Spirit of truth, comes, He will guide you into all the truth; for He will not speak on His own initiative, but whatever He hears, He will speak; and He will disclose to you what is to come' (NASB).

> Everything Jesus had to say to his church was put into print in the twenty-seven books of the New Testament, and there it ends.

Jesus was explaining how his ascension to the Father would be for the advantage of the church because it would ensure the coming of the Holy Spirit. 'But I tell you the truth, it is to your advantage that I go away; for if I do not go away, the Helper shall not come to you; but if I go, I will send Him to you' (v. 7). As well as bringing sinners to conviction (v. 8) the Spirit would provide the finishing touches to revelation, so that at long last the people of God would have 'all the truth'. The disciples were promised that the Holy Spirit 'will guide you into all the truth'. We are not entitled to wrench this promise from its context.

This work of the Holy Spirit cannot be legitimately pushed beyond the apostolic age. It is not still going on today! We are not still in the process of being 'guided into all the truth'. How do we know? By observing proper principles of interpretation. Jesus made this promise to a specific audience, his small band of Jewish disciples living around A.D. 30. *They* were about to be cast out of synagogues and killed (v. 2). *They* were in no fit state to hear the extra truths that Jesus wished to tell them because *they* were depressed that he was going away (vv. 6 & 12). Jesus made the promise to that precise group of followers. *They* would receive the full disclosures of the Holy Spirit. *They* would be told all that Christ wanted the church to know. To *them* would come 'all the truth'. Jesus was talking to them in Israel in the first half of the first century, not to us all over the world early in the twenty-first century.

The critical question is: Did Jesus keep his promise? Did the church, prior to the death of the last Apostle (John) come to possess 'all the truth'? Did the Holy Spirit 'deliver the goods'? Yes, and those 'goods' are preserved in the full New Testament writings, given under supervision of the Spirit. The phrase 'He will guide you into all the truth' refers to the inspiration of the New Testament writings, finished around A.D. 90 in the Book of Revelation. In that process the Holy Spirit finished the task indicated: 'He will disclose to you what is to come.' The term 'all the truth' amounts to 'all Scripture', namely the sixty-six canonical books.

If anyone argues that the church is still being led into 'all the truth' they are burdened with the conclusion that Jesus did not keep his word then, and that at no stage does the church have 'all the truth'. Even 2,000 years later we are still allegedly receiving updates. Worse, even they are lost for ever, 'blowing in the wind'. The whole notion is untenable.

Also untenable is the charge of 'limiting God', as if putting a limit on revelation is putting limits on God. But this is not so. Even on purely rational grounds the charge fails. Why should it be a limitation on God to say that he has spoken so plainly and fully in the sixty-six books that he will speak no more? Indeed if God needs to keep speaking in every age, in every land, and in every church, we might well think he is limited. If God speaks year after year, never fully expressing his mind, always adding, always supplementing, never reaching completion or sufficiency or perfection, the notion of a limited God might be raised with some justification.

Upon examination, it is 'ongoing revelation' that implies a limited view of God. The historic Christian view gives greater glory to God. We do not marvel that he has finished speaking. Rather, we marvel that he was willing to speak so long, so often, so repeatedly, and so fully as he did. God is not a 'talk-fest'. He does not speak incessantly, as one with limitations might do.

This notion of ongoing revelation is the *scandal* of the church today. All over the world there are self-styled 'prophets' claiming God has given messages to them. It is irrelevant whether they call it tongues, or 'words of knowledge', or the leading of the Spirit, or any other name. The bottom line is the same. They claim God is still telling them his will. They claim to have supplementary information on God's will beyond the 'hard copy' (the Bible). This is the first and foremost characteristic of every cult, with no exceptions.

All sects and cults have their own sources of extra-biblical revelation. The Adventists have Ellen G. White, the Watchtower Society has Charles Taze Russell, and the Mormons have Brigham Young. The cult known as the 'People's Temple' was so fanatically convinced by their guru Jim Jones that 911 of them drank cyanide in a mass suicide in Guyana on 20 November 1978. Whether it is David Koresh (Branch Davidian cult), David Berg (Children of God cult), Marshall Applewhite (Heaven's Gate cult), or Sun Myung Moon (Unification cult), they all start with claims of new revelation from God outside the Bible.

This same error plagued the early Gnostics, the Montanists, the Anabaptists and the Quakers, and it drives the modern charismatic movement. Whatever form it takes in history it is a dangerous error. It is not orthodox Christianity. Our guidance is the unique, finished, hard copy known as Holy Scripture. It is perfect, God-breathed, and sufficient to equip believers 'for every good work'. It needs no supplementation. It has no gaps to be filled with extras from heaven. These are the facts of historic Christianity.

## Questions

1. *To what extent is Psalm 19 a commentary on both natural revelation (vv. 1-6) and special revelation (vv. 7-14)?*

2. *'Good guidance depends on a good knowledge of Christ.' Is that a fair conclusion from Colossians 2:2-7?*

3. *How do the following texts encourage us to rest on Scripture alone as our guide for life? (John 15:9-16; 2 Peter 1:3-6; and 1 John 2:3-6.)*

# 8. God has spoken fully
## The historical proof

*Please read: Acts 17:1-15*

To say that God has spoken fully is no small claim. Whether people agree or disagree, there are massive implications for both the *style* and the *content* of their Christianity. It is time to consider the rationale for this doctrine of the cessation of revelation and sufficiency of Scripture. We need to be very clear on what the topic is, namely: *Does* God still speak to us? Are there still new words of revelation coming from God? Is God still directly talking to people today like he did to prophets like Moses and Jeremiah, and to apostles like Peter and Paul? Is God still telling us things we need to know in order to obey his will?

The question is not '*Can* God still speak to us?' Or 'Is it possible?' That has never been debated. It is certainly possible for God to continue speaking if he wishes. It is also possible for him to create another universe if he wishes. But just as surely as

God has ceased from creating universes, he has also ceased from revealing his will. Three main lines of evidence deserve our attention. It is convenient to refer to them as the historical proof, the biblical proof and the theological proof. This chapter considers the first (historical) evidence for ceased revelation.

From time to time there have been those who have denied this, and claimed they were still getting messages from God. But they have always been fringe groups teaching sectarian and unorthodox novelties. They include the Gnostics of the first century, the Montanists in the second century, the Medieval Mystics, Pietists and Quietists in the seventeenth century, the Anabaptists in post-Reformation times, and the Quakers. The charismatic movement is a modern example. Over and over again mainstream Christianity has refuted their dangerous views. We will consider the testimony of:

1. The Protestant creeds
2. The post-apostolic leaders

## The Protestant creeds

It is a sobering fact that the great Protestant creeds hold exactly the same view of revelation as the *Westminster Confession*. They include the *French Confession 1559,* the *Belgic Confession 1561,* the *2nd Helvetic Confession 1566,* the *39 Articles of the Church of England 1571,* the *Irish Articles of Religion 1615,* the *Scottish Confession of Faith 1560,* and the *Baptist Confession of Faith 1689* (subscribed to by Charles Spurgeon). More recently two other important documents have emerged, *The*

*Chicago Statement on Biblical Inerrancy 1978,* drawn up by a body of 300 international evangelical scholars from across the Protestant denominations, and *The Chicago Statement on Biblical Hermeneutics 1982* (made by over 100 international evangelical scholars). They embrace the same doctrine as the creeds, namely the exclusive, supreme, sufficient revelation of Scripture. They not only uphold this doctrine, but also explain many true and false implications. Consider the following small sample of the historical documents.

- *Belgic Confession 1561*

     Holy Scripture contains the will of God *completely* and ... everything one must believe to be saved is sufficiently taught in it. For since the *entire manner of service* which God requires of us is described in it at great length, no one — even an apostle or an angel from heaven ... ought to teach other than what the Holy Scriptures have already taught us. For since it is forbidden to add to or subtract from the Word of God, this plainly demonstrates that the teaching is *perfect and complete* in all respects.

     Therefore we must not consider human writing — no matter how holy their authors may have been — equal to the divine writings; nor may we put custom, nor the majority, nor age, nor the passage of time or persons, nor councils, decrees, or official decisions above the truth of God, for truth is above everything else. For all human beings are liars by nature and more vain than vanity itself. Therefore we reject with all our hearts everything that does not agree with this infallible rule.

- *2nd Helvetic Confession 1566* (Swiss Protestants)

  Scripture teaches *fully* all goodness ... in this Holy
  Scripture the universal church of Christ has the most
  *complete* exposition of *all* that pertains to a saving faith,
  and also to the framing of a life acceptable to God: and
  in this respect it is expressly commanded by God that
  nothing either be added to or taken from the same ...
  neither any other word of God is to be invented (feigned,
  pretended) *nor is it to be expected* from heaven.

- *Irish Articles of Religion 1615*

  The Holy Scriptures contain all things necessary to
  salvation, and are able to instruct *sufficiently in all points*
  of faith that we are bound to believe, and *all good duties*
  that we are bound to practise.

The doctrine of Scripture in the *Baptist Confession of Faith
1689* retains the same words as the *Westminster Confession*
on which it is based. An interesting creed is the *London Baptist
Confession of 1644*. It was drawn up by seven congregations in
London as a way of utterly repudiating any connection with the
Anabaptist sect. The London Baptists believed in the cessation
of revelation and the sufficiency of Scripture, but they tired of
being falsely mixed up with Anabaptists who denied it. Among
other things, this creed says:

  In this written word, God has plainly revealed
  *whatsoever* He has thought *needful* for us to know,

believe and acknowledge ... the role of knowledge, faith and obedience, concerning the worship and service of God and *all other Christian duties*, is not man's inventions, opinions, devices, laws, constitutions, or traditions unwritten whatsoever, but *only* the word of God contained in Canonical Scriptures.

So here is the unambiguous voice of Protestant Evangelical churches from France, Scotland, the Netherlands, England, Switzerland, Ireland and America. It is an international voice. Here are the voices of Presbyterians, Anglicans, Baptists and others, all saying exactly the same thing: *God has spoken fully!* There is no more revelation to be given from heaven! If you are still hearing voices from heaven it is a figment of your imagination! God has finished speaking!

*A scandal to avoid*

The scandal of the modern church, even within the ranks of the denominations above, is that many people are ignorant of their heritage. Despising their birthright, they are running after extra revelations, and turning their backs on their forefathers who were prepared to die for these very truths. Guido de Bres, chief author of the *Belgic Confession*, did actually die as a martyr. The original petitioners placed

> The scandal of the modern church is that many people are ignorant of their heritage ... turning their backs on their forefathers who were prepared to die for these very truths.

that confession before King Phillip II of the Netherlands. Rather than deny the truths expressed in this confession, they declared they would 'offer their backs to stripes, their tongues to knives, their mouths to gags, and their whole bodies to the fire'. Thousands suffered exactly those sorts of persecutions. It is profoundly disturbing that their blood is considered so cheap today.

It is not hard to find modern churches ignorant of their historical roots, and carelessly indifferent towards all things old. Unhealthy individualism has produced modern Christians who are still beguiled by the serpent's cynical question: 'Indeed, has God said?' (Genesis 3:1, NASB). They are running back to the ancient lie that Scripture is not enough. They are swamped in the sea of subjectivism and extra verbal guidance. Satan doesn't care whether it is called the Infallible Magisterium of the Vatican, or tongues, or prophecy, or 'the inner voice of God speaking to me'. It is the same old denial of the sufficiency of Scripture. Paul's words to the Galatians are particularly apt here: 'You foolish Galatians, who has bewitched you?' (3:1).

## The post-apostolic leaders

Try to imagine what it was like to live at the end of the first century, to have actually seen the Apostles, spoken with them, heard them preach and been instructed by them. Imagine having attended their funerals.

We do not need to imagine it because we have the writings of the Christian leaders who were in exactly that situation, men like Clement, Ignatius and Polycarp. The question of whether

God had finished speaking would have been very real to them. They knew he had continued speaking inspired revelations through the Apostles. They acknowledged their writings as God's word, but now that they were dead and buried, had God finished speaking? Had his word been fully revealed or could they expect the flow of revelation to be ongoing? Would there be new revelations of the Spirit, or was Scripture sufficient for all faith and life?

They answered in the same way as the later creeds. Revelation has ceased with the last of the Apostles. A quote from each of these three men will be helpful.

*Clement of Rome* (circa A.D. 95). According to the evidence available, Clement had seen the Apostles and regarded them highly. He wrote: 'The Apostles received the gospel for us from the Lord Jesus Christ ... so they are ... the greatest and most righteous pillars of the Church.' His point is that the Apostles were direct recipients of gospel revelation. They were inspired, getting their revelations directly from the Holy Spirit. All the rest of us (Clement too) are indirect recipients of that revelation, not its original agents. So Clement says of the apostle Paul, 'Truly, under the inspiration of the Spirit, he wrote to you.'

*Ignatius of Antioch* wrote at about A.D. 117. In a very humble way he spoke about not being 'competent for this, being a convict, that I should write to you as though I were an Apostle ... I do not, as Peter and Paul, issue commandments unto you. They were Apostles. I am but a condemned man.' He not only distinguished himself from the Apostles who no longer existed, but he also made it very clear that divine revelations ceased with them. Ignatius simply writes as an ordinary man whose words (though wise) are inferior to revelation.

*Polycarp* wrote at the same time – A.D. 118. He is particularly interesting because Irenaus the historian tells us he was a pupil of the Apostles and had been sitting under their instructions. The Apostles appointed Polycarp overseer (bishop) of the Church of Smyrna. He wrote, 'For neither am I, nor is any other like unto me, able to follow the wisdom of the blessed and glorious Paul, who when he came among you, taught face to face with the men of that day the word which concerneth truth carefully and surely, who also, when he was absent, wrote a letter unto you.'

Polycarp's point is that inspired revelation has ceased, and so has the apostolic ability to teach and explain it without error. When the Apostles preached Christ as the fulfilment of the Old Testament Scriptures, their messages were just as much inspired and authoritative as the permanent record of them (the New Testament writings). But both have ceased. Polycarp insisted there was no succession of the gift of revelation beyond the Apostles, not even to men they instructed face-to-face and appointed to church leadership! The writings of the other church leaders of those days, like Papias (A.D. 140), Diognetus and Barnabas, make the same points.

## Conclusion

For any unbiased mind, these historic facts speak loud and clear. Here were men who could very easily and plausibly have claimed 'ongoing revelations'. They personally knew the Apostles and it would not have been difficult for them to claim that God continued to speak through them. They were undeniably the true 'successors' of the Apostles, in the sense of being the next generation of leaders, preachers and theologians. They were learned, scholarly men, and gifted communicators who could have raised convincing arguments to support any claims of new revelations of the Spirit. They would have been formidable opponents for anyone seeking to differ with them.

If ever the time was conducive for new revelations, it was right there and then, while the Apostles still lived and preached, while inspired revelation and authoritative interpretation and counsel was still coming from God. It was a very practical issue for them. Could they stand up in their pulpits and say, like Paul, 'This revelation I received from the Lord'? Was God still speaking through them like he was through the Apostles? Could they write in their letters, 'Thus says the Lord' in the primary and direct sense that the prophets did? Their answer was strongly negative. Repeatedly and consistently they denied that God was still speaking. If anything is clear from these writings, it is that there are no more Apostles, no more revelations, and no more infallible and authoritative messages from God.

The Word of God is completed in the apostolic writings, the twenty-seven canonical books. Together with the thirty-nine books of the Old Testament, these sixty-six books provide the total, clear and sufficient revelation of God's will for his church. The Bible is absolutely perfect, lacking nothing, equipping every believer for 'every good work'. Beyond that nothing is to be expected, pretended or added.

There is a bird's-eye view of church history. In different countries over many centuries the church has repeatedly confessed the cessation of revelation. *Has God spoken fully?* The historical facts answer the question plainly: *Yes he has!* Do not be apologetic about it! Do not ever forget it! Do not be open to claims of ongoing revelation. Do not trample underfoot the blood of the martyrs! Let us not participate in the scandal of the modern church. Let us rejoice at the sufficiency of Scripture and study to know it better!

## Questions

1. *From Acts 17:11, exactly what is the 'noble character' shown in Berea, and what does it imply about guidance today?*

2. *'I have more insight than all my teachers, for I meditate on your statutes' (Psalm 119:99). How can that be true without arrogance?*

3. *How can the psalmist imply (in Psalm 119:11) that Scripture is a sufficient guide against all wrong behaviour, when much more Scripture had yet to be revealed?*

# 9. God has spoken fully
## *The biblical proof*

*Please read: Revelation 22:12-21*

N ow we take up the second line of proof for the cessation of revelation, the biblical proof. Two key texts are far richer than is often appreciated (2 Timothy 3:16-17 and Revelation 22:18). Together they declare some important observations about revelation, namely:

1. Additions are unnecessary
2. Additions are cursed


**Additions are unnecessary** (2 Timothy 3:16-17)

'All Scripture is God-breathed and is useful for teaching, rebuking, correcting and training in righteousness, so that the man of God may be thoroughly equipped for every good work.'

Two important questions need to be answered here. What is Paul talking about when he uses the term 'all Scripture', and what are the claims he is making about it?

*What is Paul talking about?*

It is often assumed that Paul must be referring exclusively to the Old Testament when he uses the term 'all Scripture' (*pasa graphe,* πᾶσα γραφη). It is also assumed that the previous verse supports that opinion. Describing Timothy it says, 'from childhood you have known the sacred writings' (NASB). Undoubtedly these 'sacred writings' refer to the Old Testament writings that Timothy had been taught by his mother Eunice and his grandmother Lois (2 Timothy 1:5).

However, it is a mistake to equate 'the sacred writings' (*hiera grammata,* ἱερὰ γράμματα) in verse 14 with 'all Scripture' in verse 15, as if both refer to the thirty-nine books of the Old Testament (see the reasons below). As a consequence of that mistake, it is argued that this text has no relevance to the question of revelation beyond Scripture because it is only talking about the Old Testament. It is alleged that, if anything, the door of ongoing revelation is left open because God *did* add more revelation to those thirty-nine books, namely the twenty-seven books of the New Testament.

Plausible as that sounds, it does not stand up to examination. There are at least four good reasons for rejecting that view. Instead we should understand 'all Scripture' to include both the Old Testament and the New Testament. These reasons amount to four interpretive tests: the substitution test, the Lukan test, the Pauline test and the Petrine test.

*1. The substitution test*

If the term 'all Scripture' is restricted to the Old Testament a real problem is introduced. Go back to the verse again, this time substituting 'the Old Testament' in place of 'all Scripture' (the alleged equivalent). It will then read: 'The Old Testament is God-breathed and is useful for teaching, rebuking, correcting and training in righteousness, so that the man of God may be thoroughly equipped for every good work.' In that case Paul is asserting that the Old Testament is a sufficient revelation of God's will. It teaches all we need to know about pleasing God in every situation in life ('for every good work').

But what does that imply for the New Testament? Were the apostolic writings necessary? Did God give us more than we need? Is the New Testament superfluous? Is there no net gain by having those twenty-seven inspired books? Is there no net loss without them? Is Paul really saying that Moses and the Prophets are quite adequate for all our needs, leaving the New Testament as the non-essential icing on the cake?

Obviously not! The New Testament is of critical importance. It provides a very big plus, a very significant advance. Whereas the Old Testament is the covenant *promise*, the New Testament is the *promise fulfilled*. The Old Testament ends *begging* for a New Testament. It ends waiting for the promised Messiah. It closes with no kingdom and no king in Israel, just a corrupt priesthood and corrupt sacrifices with a little faithful remnant longing for the promised kingdom to come, waiting for David's Son. The Jewish scriptures close with the prediction of a great High Priest who will cleanse the temple and purify the sons of Levi like a fuller's soap. The Old Testament ends in suspense, waiting for a perfect sacrifice, a Lamb of God without blemish, who takes away all the sins of the people.

And that is exactly where the New Testament begins. After a cessation of revelation for 400 years, the gospel announces: 'The kingdom of God is at hand'; 'Behold the lamb of God who takes away the sin of the world.' The New Testament is the key that unlocks the Old Testament. It shows how prophecy is to be understood, how it all relates to Christ and his church. The New Testament is the Holy Spirit's interpretation of the Old Testament. Without it we would have no idea of which Jewish laws still applied now that Messiah has come, and which laws do not apply. Confusion would reign regarding theocracy, ceremonies, Levites, Passover, circumcision, food laws, clean and unclean animals, temple taxes, grain offerings, heave offerings, whole burnt offerings, and many other things. So Paul's term 'all Scripture' does not refer exclusively to the Old Testament! It does not fit the context.

In fact, by contrast, it will be seen that Paul really makes a far smaller claim for the Old Testament Scriptures in the previous verse. He claims that they were sufficient for something very important, namely making a man wise enough to put his faith in Christ for salvation: 'from childhood you have known the sacred writings which are able to give you the wisdom that leads to salvation through faith which is in Christ Jesus'. But the claims of the next verse extend way beyond that. 'All

∞∞∞∞∞∞∞∞∞∞∞∞∞∞∞∞∞

'All Scripture' not only leads you to Christ, but it thoroughly equips you for every decision you make after you have become a Christian.

∞∞∞∞∞∞∞∞∞∞∞∞∞∞∞∞∞

Scripture' not only leads you to Christ, but it thoroughly equips you for every decision you make after you have become a Christian.

## 2. The Lukan test

Paul describes Luke's writing as 'Scripture'. In 1 Timothy 5:18 he uses this word 'Scripture' with the definite article (the Scripture, ἡ γραφή): 'For the Scripture says, "Do not muzzle the ox while it is treading out the grain," and "The worker deserves his wages".' He is quoting two writings here. The first comes as no surprise, namely Deuteronomy 25:4 (Old Testament). But the second is especially interesting because it is a quote from Luke's Gospel (Luke 10:7).

This proves not only that Luke's Gospel was in circulation but also that it was already accepted as 'Scripture', having an equal status with Moses and the Prophets. So the Apostle quotes both Old and New Testament texts alongside each other and labels them jointly as 'the Scripture'. That has a major implication.

Since Paul uses the term *'the* Scripture' to include some New Testament writings, when he later uses the term *'all* Scripture' he must mean the sum total of all those writings which can legitimately be called 'Scripture'. In other words, he must mean all the true Old Testament and New Testament writings! So it is wrong to restrict the word 'Scripture' only to the Old Testament. That opinion is disqualified by Paul's use of the word. Nothing is altered by the fact that the full New Testament was not then available (indeed Paul himself was still writing the biggest part of it). Regardless of when the ink dried on the New Testament writings, they belong to 'the Scripture' as Paul understood that term. At the end of the day, whatever finally lays legitimate claim to be 'God-breathed writing' is included in the term 'all Scripture'. It must include the twenty-seven New Testament books.

### 3. The Pauline test

It is very clear that Paul regarded his own teachings as equal to anything in the Old Testament, being fully inspired and authoritative. Notice what he said to Timothy in verse 14: 'But as for you, continue in what you have learned and have become convinced of, because you know those from whom you learned it.' What is it that Timothy has 'learned and become convinced of'? And from whom did he learn it? Who is this teacher and what is this teaching?

The answer must embrace what immediately follows: 'useful for teaching, rebuking, correcting and training in righteousness, so that the man of God may be thoroughly equipped for every good work'. It has to accord with 'all Scripture is God-breathed'. There is no doubt at all what the answer is. Paul is referring to himself as an inspired Apostle, and to the teachings he has already passed on to Timothy, including what Luke wrote. Some other Pauline texts confirm this.

'I am writing you these instructions so that … you will know how people ought to conduct themselves in God's household, which is the church of the living God, the pillar and foundation of the truth' (1 Timothy 3:14-15). Since Paul insists that his writings and instructions are needful to equip the church for every good work, they must be a part of 'all Scripture'.

'And the things you have heard me say in the presence of many witnesses entrust to reliable men who will also be qualified to teach others... Keep reminding them of these things' (2 Timothy 2:2, 14). These are things God wants them to know, things profitable for teaching, correction and training in righteousness. They too have the status of 'Scripture'.

'What you heard from me, keep as the pattern of sound teaching, with faith and love in Christ Jesus. Guard the good deposit that was entrusted to you — guard it with the help of the Holy Spirit who lives in us' (2 Timothy 1:13-14). Clearly Paul regards his own apostolic teaching in exactly the same way he regards the Old Testament writings. The entire product is 'the pattern of sound teaching' to be guarded by the help of the Holy Spirit. So it is not just Deuteronomy and Luke's Gospel that Paul denotes by the term 'all Scripture'. He also includes his own apostolic teachings.

This is supported by his words to the Corinthians: 'If anybody thinks he is a prophet or spiritually gifted, let him acknowledge that what I am writing to you is the Lord's command' (1 Corinthians 14:37). There can be no debate here. Since Paul's writing 'is the Lord's command' it is nothing less than Scripture. And, if further proof is needed: 'I want you to know, brothers, that the gospel I preached is not something that man made up. I did not receive it from any man, nor was I taught it; rather, I received it by revelation from Jesus Christ' (Galatians 1:11-12). Paul's preached message is nothing less than direct revelation from Jesus Christ, so it must be described as 'Scripture' and 'God-breathed'. If anyone still refuses to accept that apostolic revelations directly from Christ belong to the term 'all Scripture', words have lost all meaning.

111

## 4. The Petrine test

The apostle Peter lays to rest all doubts about this matter. 'Our dear brother Paul also wrote to you with the wisdom that God gave him. He writes the same way in all his letters, speaking in them of these matters. His letters contain some things that are hard to understand, which ignorant and unstable people distort, as they do the other Scriptures, to their own destruction' (2 Peter 3:15-16). Peter's complaint is not that ignorant men misuse Paul's writings and they misuse Scripture (as if there are two classes of writing here). Rather, what they do to Paul's writings they also do to 'the other Scriptures' (τὰς λοιπὰς γραφὰς). There is only one class of writing here, the Scriptures. There are the Scriptures that Paul wrote and the Scriptures that Moses and others wrote, but they all constitute the one revelation of God.

How does all this prove that there are no more revelations today? The answer is evident in the claims Paul now makes about Scripture.

## What claims is Paul making about Scripture?

Three different descriptions are piled up here to underline the wonderful sufficiency of Scripture: *complete* (ἄρτιος), *thoroughly equipped* (ἐξηρτισμένος), and *every good work* (πᾶν ἔργον ἀγαθὸν). God's people do not have just enough revelation in the Bible to 'get by'. On the contrary, we have enough to be *complete!* We are not just 'reasonably equipped' but *thoroughly equipped!* Scripture does not teach us what we need for 'most good works' but for *every good work.*

If this means anything, it means that when the Scriptures were finished, revelation for this age was completed. That needs underscoring. Here is the death and burial of 'ongoing revelation'. Since Scripture lacks nothing, there is no logic in further revelations. Paul could not be more emphatic. There is no way to insist on extra revelations without coming unstuck on the doctrine of Scripture. Intended or not, new revelations imply inadequacies in the old revelations. But Scripture is a perfectly adequate statement of God's will, equipping us for every good work. Therefore additions are unnecessary.

## Additions are cursed (Revelation 22:18)

'I warn everyone who hears the words of the prophecy of this book: If anyone adds anything to them, God will add to him the plagues described in this book.'

It is very simplistic to think this warning only applies to tampering with John's book, the Apocalypse. That would leave John saying in effect: 'This book starts at chapter 1 verse 1 and ends at chapter 22 verse 21, so don't add a verse 22! Don't add another sentence, or even another word, to my Patmos prophecy!' Obviously he includes that idea, but he would not tolerate anyone tampering with any other part of Scripture either. We cannot have John implying that, so long as you leave this book alone, feel free to add extra things to the writings of Moses, or the Psalms, or Amos, or even John's other biblical texts (his three letters and Gospel). The same jealousy he has for one part of Scripture must be applied to all Scripture.

Does this mean that, for someone wishing to add new revelations, the only option left is to go outside Scripture? Is John implying that you are cursed if you add to the sixty-six canonical books, but please feel free to add other revelations externally? Play safe, avoid the curse, and insist you are not adding *to* Scripture, rather you are placing new revelations of the Spirit *alongside* of Scripture? No, of course not, and to understand why that is so, an important feature of this book of Revelation needs to be appreciated. It is critical for understanding the issue here.

Of all the books in the Bible, this last one especially manifests the family tree. It cannot be seen in isolation from the other sixty-five books. This book is most comprehensively married to the Old Testament books. It is absolutely impossible to understand John without a good prior knowledge of the Old Testament, especially Genesis, Ezekiel, Daniel and Isaiah. Many of John's symbols are taken from these places. John reaches far back into Old Testament prophecy and shows how the key ideas integrate in Christ and his church. The two prophetic 'moments' (the ancient Old Testament moment and the recent New Testament moment) are wedded together as husband and wife. The two have become one flesh. They are joined and shall never be divorced! John is the one who traces the essential oneness of the two testaments from their very beginning to their eternal consummation. In other words, he traces the union between the bridegroom (Christ) and his bride (the Church) from the start of history to its end.

Therefore, what John calls 'the words of the prophecy of this book' *cannot* refer only to the words he penned as distinct from the words of Moses, Ezekiel, Isaiah, David, Daniel and the others he frequently incorporates. Their prophecies and John's words are now one united whole. They are fused to form one message, one ultimate meaning, one volume, one 'revelation', and one whole 'word of God'. Now they all make sense in Christ who reigns as King of kings and Lord of lords. That is precisely the significance of his words in 22:13: 'I am the Alpha and the Omega, the First and the Last, the Beginning and the End.'

John has gathered up all time (past, present and future), showing that Christ is central throughout. Jesus is the interpreter of all events just as the alphabet (Alpha to Omega) is needed to interpret every word. Jesus is the complete key to all meaning. You need no more because there is no more. Adding new revelations is analogous to adding new letters to the alphabet. It makes no sense.

So John's phrase 'the words of the prophecy of this book' must be taken in the most comprehensive sense. It refers not merely to John's own words, but also to those of Moses, David, Ezekiel, Daniel and Isaiah. John adopts their words and symbols as his own in order to explain Christ. Ultimately John's term 'the words of the prophecy of this book' is as broad as Paul's 'all Scripture'. The sum total of all true prophetic utterance is complete. The whole revelation of God (for which Jesus is the 'yes and amen') has come. These 'sacred writings' need no supplementation in any shape or form. Such additions are cursed!

Those who claim new revelations are in danger of placing themselves under the curse! They are inviting the plagues of this book. It is a serious thing to be a false prophet. It is a serious thing to say God told you something when he didn't.

It is a serious thing for anyone to promote himself as a link between God and men. It is a serious thing to insist that people should listen to what God 'told' you as well as what God told Moses. It is a serious thing to imply that having the Bible is not enough revelation. And these serious things apply to all who have the audacity to claim God is still speaking to them. May God turn them from the folly of their way before the curse falls with dreadful finality.

## Questions

1. *In what ways has John drawn on the original home of God's people (Eden) for his description of their final home (the New Jerusalem)? Read Genesis 2 and Revelation 21.*

2. *'True disciples can be very misguided if Christ is not their interpretive key.' Is this a fair conclusion from Luke 24:13-53?*

3. *What logic explains how a law about animals can validly apply to men? (Compare Deuteronomy 25:4 and 1 Timothy 5:8.)*

# 10. God has spoken fully
## The theological proof

*Please read: Psalm 119:169-176*

We turn now to the *theological proof* for the sufficiency of Scripture. Even more than the other modes of enquiry, theology forces us to think in terms of the bigger picture. Whereas historical proof concerns itself with historical facts, and biblical proof concerns itself with textual facts, theology embraces both of them, along with other fields of learning, to give us the most panoramic view. Theology provides us with some additional reasons for rejecting the claims of ongoing revelation. They can be summarized in the following three ways.

1. The problem of no brakes
2. The problem of blind faith
3. The problem of lost property

## The problem of no brakes

An illustration will help show the problem of ongoing revelations. Suppose you are setting out on a long journey, a car trip with your family to a distant holiday place. It will take several days, though the children will soon be asking 'How long before we get there?' You tell them it is a long way off but every hour brings them nearer. Everyone is looking forward to arriving at the destination. As you drive, the sense of progress heightens. Key landmarks are registered as you pass towns, mountains and rivers. But it is still too early to find your destination named on road signs.

Eventually it does appear on the occasional sign (even if it indicates hundreds of kilometres). There is a new optimism. Soon your destination occurs more frequently on the signs until it becomes the main one. Finally you arrive at your promised rest. Your hopes are realized and your satisfaction is complete. At last the car can stop. There are no more milestones and no more messages on road signs. There is no more progress to make. At last you can enjoy having arrived. At last Dad can put the brakes on.

Can you imagine the outrage if the driver decided to keep on going? Imagine him saying, 'I'm getting used to this travel ... I like the idea of seeing new messages and road signs every day ... we've been doing it so long now it seems a shame to stop ... I don't think I could cope without new signs ... I don't like the idea of arriving at a destination ... I don't like the idea of rejoicing in a completed journey or soaking up success ... I don't think I could cope with a holiday ... let's keep on trucking!' So he continues driving, and every minute takes you further and further from the original goal. In fact the very idea of 'goal' or 'destination' loses meaning. It fades in the rear-view mirror.

Biblical revelation progresses like that holiday trip. It moves in an orderly way from elementary to advanced; from shadow to substance; from promise to fulfilment; from seed to full-grown tree. It is never the opposite way, never regressive. The Bible moves forward, like an arrow to its target. Beyond dispute that target is Christ. Everything in Moses and the Prophets and the Psalms climaxes in Christ (Luke 24:44). The whole Old Testament aims at Jesus (John 5:39). He is God's final word, the climax of all revelation (Hebrews 1:1-2).

Progress can progress no further. The arrow has reached its mark and rests from its flight. God has fully revealed the 'good news'. There is no other news. God has given us the final chapter. God rests his case in the revelation of his Son. There is nothing more to say. There is nothing more that can be said. Jesus is the ultimate demonstration of God's love and the ultimate statement of God's word. God's final statement is essentially, 'This is my Son, whom I love. Listen to him!' (Mark 9:7). There can be no progress beyond that. The brakes have been applied to revelation.

It is ignorance of this vital theological truth that drives the vehicle of 'ongoing revelation'. It is regressive, taking the church back into pre-Christian modes, reversing the whole direction of biblical disclosure. It is committing the very sin that the book of Hebrews was written to prevent, the sin of returning to temporary and elementary things, going back into the shadows, back to weak and obsolete things. The Bible has lifted us to the highest point of God's revelation. Beyond that peak it is all downhill. Why go back to prophets and mediators when the great Prophet and Mediator has come? Why go back to messages from God when God's ultimate message has appeared in the flesh?

Belief in ongoing revelation is as foolish as driving past your holiday destination. If no brake has been applied to revelation the machine still rolls on. Where? Why? There is no sensible answer. The whole idea of being complete in Christ is lost. The whole idea of a sufficient revelation of God's will, in which we can rest our case and enjoy our inheritance, is lost by those who 'keep on trucking' more messages from heaven. Like a five-star holiday unit, the Bible is fully furnished with everything we need. It is profitable for teaching, correcting and training us, so that every one taking refuge under its roof is 'fully equipped for every good work'.

We cannot have it both ways! We are either confidently resting in Scripture alone or are busy looking elsewhere. We are either enjoying the promised rest in Christ, the goal and climax of all revelation, or we have ignored it and are moving further and further away. We either applied the brakes where all orthodox theology does (at Revelation 22:21) or we still have our foot on the accelerator. Like Israel in the wilderness, we expect ongoing daily supplies of manna (food from heaven). We need to understand that Christ has brought us into the Promised Land 'flowing with milk and honey'. The manna is beyond its

> We need to understand that Christ has brought us into the Promised Land 'flowing with milk and honey'.

'use-by' date and has stopped falling from heaven. It is a mark of immaturity to look for ongoing supplies.

## The problem of blind faith

When any person claims new revelation from God, a major problem arises, namely the problem of *subjectivity*. The realm of perceptions and subjective experiences lies beyond the reach of verification. We cannot prove our inner experiences and no one can disprove them. What I experience, I experience. I may as well say, 'I had a dream', as say, 'I had a revelation.' Both are unproved and unprovable. When someone claims God spoke to him, the question of credibility arises. Why should you believe it? Without the support of objective facts, to accept that claim is mere blind faith.

In the case of true prophets, God overcame that problem by giving them miraculous signs and wonders as authentication. These supernatural powers were their *ID papers*. God stamped his approval on them, making it clear that he had truly spoken to them, obliging others to listen and obey their message. The signs of Moses, the signs of the Apostles and the signs of Jesus compelled faith in their messages. But those signs have ceased. Of course God still does great works, but they are not 'signs' in the biblical sense. They do not authenticate an inspired agent of revelation. We must resist the common misuse of the word 'miracle'.

To illustrate the problem of blind faith, imagine the following dialogue taking place between two church members, Jack and Jill:

**Jack:** I had a revelation from God last night.

**Jill:** No, you didn't Jack, revelations ceased with the full Bible.

**Jack:** I know what I heard. God spoke to me as certainly as you spoke to me just now.

**Jill:** No doubt you experienced something, Jack, but you have interpreted it wrongly.

**Jack:** How dare you say I got it wrong! I should know! I'm the one it happened to! How can you be so dogmatic? On what basis do you say I got it wrong?

**Jill:** On the basis of correct Bible teaching, orthodox Christian theology. Our preacher has given some sermons on this very thing, showing us that God has spoken fully in the Bible. We have seen the historical proof, the biblical proof and the theological proof. The true church has always denied ongoing revelation. It typifies sects and cults like Gnostics, Montanists, Mystics and Quakers.

**Jack:** That's too bad, because God did speak to me and I'm not in a cult!

**Jill:** Okay, then, show me where all the Protestant creeds got it wrong! And show me where our preacher interpreted the Bible wrongly, because he convinced me from the key texts. Let's go through his exegesis step by step and show me where he went wrong.

**Jack:** That's your problem Jill, you are too intellectual. You are just too logical for your own good. Christianity is not meant to be so doctrinally precise as that. You treat the Bible as if it is to be the final judge of all acts and opinions. You wave it around like a sword! Loosen up, Jill, get your head out of the printed pages and be open to the leading of the Holy Spirit. Let go and let God! Let God speak his new revelations to you! Stop judging me with the Bible and the history of orthodox theology. I don't care if all the great creeds and theologians disagree with me. That's their problem not mine. All I know is that God spoke to me.

**Jill:** So, Jack, you are saying the whole army is out of step except you. Doesn't that worry you?

**Jack:** What worries me, Jill, is that you are so objective that you are in danger of resisting God's Spirit. You put so much importance on objective, grammatical biblical facts that you are not 'open'. You leave no room for faith.

**Jill:** I have faith in everything God says in his word, and in all the proper inferences flowing from it. But true faith is reasonable, not blind faith like yours, Jack. You let your feelings and experiences govern your faith. That's why you believe in these ongoing revelations. I fear that you are a mystic, Jack. I can't reason with you because you have already consigned logical reasoning to the dustbin. You don't care that the most gifted thinkers and writers disagree with you. You think it nothing that the most learned synods and councils in church history say you're wrong. You won't devote one minute to showing where their interpretation of Scripture is faulty. You look down on the enlightened church with a haughty air of piety, puffed up in your assurance that God has spoken privately to you. You take comfort that if only they had been in your shoes ... if only God had spoken to them as he did to you, they would understand. Your unspoken prayer for them is 'Father, forgive them for they know not what they do.'

As you can imagine, the conversation goes on and on. But there is a better speech for Jill that will end the discussion very quickly.

**Jack:** I had a revelation from God last night.

**Jill:** I had a revelation from God this morning in which he told me you would say that, but he said I'm not to believe you because it didn't happen.

*Fight fire with fire!* Fight subjective nonsense with more of the same. Now Jack is faced with the same sort of mystical claims he had promoted. He cannot prove or disprove Jill's claims. She is asking for the same 'blind faith' response that he required of her. If he refuses to believe her 'revelation' he must accept her right to deny his 'revelation'. Otherwise he has to admit he is wrong.

## The problem of lost property

Since revelation is valuable property, God has taken special care to ensure that it never becomes lost property. He has preserved it in writing (hard copy). The critical importance of this fact explains why the *Westminster Confession of Faith* puts it first (1:1):

> It pleased the Lord, at different times, and in various ways, to reveal Himself, and to declare His will to His church. Afterwards, for the better preserving and spreading of the truth, and for the more sure establishment and comfort of the church against the corruption of the flesh, and the malice of Satan and of the world, God committed the same wholly unto writing. This makes the Holy Scripture therefore essential because God's former ways of revealing His will to His people have ceased.

The words 'wholly unto writing' (with emphasis on 'wholly') should be carefully understood. The Westminster Assembly was well aware that revelation existed in both oral and written forms during biblical times. But that does not mean God had two wills, two words, or two revelations. The oral and written forms constituted one harmonious divine revelation. There was considerable overlap between these forms of revelation (a feature still evident in the Bible). What God told Moses was repeated, enlarged and applied by the Prophets. But an inevitable historical problem had to be solved.

Security for the oral revelation grew more risky with the passage of time, yet the church had an increasing need for certainty. Apart from human corruption, the ceaseless malice of Satan and the world made it vital to have a sure and certain account of everything God wanted the church to know and teach. Therefore God in his wisdom ensured it was fully committed to writing. The formerly oral portions became hard copy. There is now only one form of revelation to guide us — the written word of God.

There was no need for every syllable of oral revelation to be preserved in writing. We know that Jesus revealed more (by miracles and words) than is found in the New Testament (John 20:30-31; 21:25). There is no record of anything said by the four daughters of Philip who 'prophesied' (Acts 21:8-9), or the oral revelations given by the prophets in Corinth (1 Corinthians 14:26-32). These sorts of omissions do not detract from the complete sufficiency of Scripture, nor do they give any credibility to further claims of oral revelation today. All the oral revelation that God wanted preserved was committed to writing. We lack nothing.

'His divine power has given us *everything* we need for life and godliness through our knowledge of him who called us by his own glory and goodness. Through these he has given us his very great and precious promises' (2 Peter 1:3-4). The essential truths of any 'non preserved' oral revelations are not lost. They are contained in the rich abundance of all that has been committed to writing. We have all the truth we need, everything God wants us to know for serving him in this age.

For many Christians this doctrine of Scripture is probably taken for granted without much thought for the process of permanently inscribing divine revelation. We have our printed Bibles. Every single word of revelation is safe and secure. Thousands of copies of the original manuscripts, and hundreds of translations into various languages, are available on computer programs, complete with powerful search engines. God's Word is very tangible, very identifiable and very concrete.

This valuable property continues to fascinate students and scholars worldwide. A huge amount of research has been done

**126**

on all manner of biblical issues. A vast and expanding archive has 'fingerprinted' the millions of details in God's Word. True revelation is *public domain* and very conspicuously so. It could not become lost property. God has well and truly seen to that. But that is not the case for other (alleged) 'revelations'.

What has become of all those supposed 'revelations' arriving daily all over the planet via numerous prophets, tongue-speakers, and other 'anointed' agents? How incongruous for those huge volumes of allegedly inspired, important and authoritative words from God to be lost to the church! They are not written down or collated or preserved or published. The church cannot study, research, or memorize these 'words of God'. They are lost property. They disappear as soon as they arrive. This is a radical and inexplicable departure from God's established way of guiding his church. It raises serious questions.

Has God now grown careless about his word? After 4,000 years of preserving every detail from Genesis to Revelation, is God unconcerned that newer revelations are lost? Why are they not preserved? Why can't I study them in detail — their nouns, verbs, participles and prepositions, even their 'jots and tittles' (Matthew 5:18)? Where can I get a copy to be edified, profited, instructed, corrected and trained for every good work (as I can with the Bible)? Why would God set his words in concrete for thousands of years only to leave any further 'revelations' blowing in the wind thereafter? Is that consistent with infinite wisdom? Of course not!

*This demands an answer!* If we still have the words spoken in the Garden of Eden, why, in this age of computers and electronic files, do we have no records of what God allegedly said this morning in New York, Toronto, or Sydney? If even a fraction of modern prophets were taken seriously, the vast quantities of claimed new revelations would fill another Bible in a single week! Apparently, guidance from heaven has really hit top gear in our age. Revelations are flooding the earth like never before. But it is all lost property. Why is nothing being done about it?

> If even a fraction of modern prophets were taken seriously, the vast quantities of claimed new revelations would fill another Bible in a single week!

What a poor attitude the Christian church is showing by treating such valuable property so carelessly, so recklessly and so flippantly. Why aren't mountains being moved to devise some system of preserving and collecting 'ongoing revelations'? And if those careless attitudes are wrong, how much worse are we in the Reformed Evangelical community? We actually *deny* those revelations! If others are reckless, we are hostile. Presumably they would call us to repent.

And suppose we do! Suppose we want to humble ourselves under God's latest 'revelations'. Suppose we want to catch up on lost time, meditating day and night in the latest counsels from heaven. We can't do it! No one can give us a copy, not even a partial or abridged edition. It is not even on the Internet, the ideal place for worldwide access and global updates. New prophets could bless the whole church by rapidly cyber-posting the latest information from heaven.

We can expose this problem by thinking a little further. If modern 'prophets' committed their revelations to writing, the 'lost property' problem would be solved. Even if just some of them co-operated it would help. But this will not happen, for at least two reasons.

1. *Because it exposes pride* (the best-case scenario). Suppose a 'prophet' is cautious enough to insist that his new revelations teach nothing different to Scripture. He says they simply bear witness to what is already in the Bible or implied by it. Will he be keen to print them? No, because he then exposes himself to a legitimate charge of arrogance. In reality he is only doing what any good preacher does, explaining the Bible and its implications for our lives. The difference is that true preachers do it without promoting themselves. They do not claim a special 'hot line' with God. They do not claim God is speaking directly with them as he did with Moses. They are expositors not revealers. At best, these modern 'prophets' are unnecessary and repetitious, but in reality they are pompous.

2. *Because it exposes error.* Suppose a 'prophet' claims God *is* telling him novel things not found or implied in Scripture. He will also be reluctant to print them because he risks being proved wrong, foolish, speculative and inconsistent. It would put him in the same class as any sect or cult. For instance, the Watchtower Society claimed that God said the world would end in 1874. When that failed they changed the date to 1914, and then to 1925. Presumably no one requires proof that they were wrong each time. Instead of admitting their error they simply readjusted the language. So it is inconvenient for modern prophets to preserve their words. It is more convenient to leave them blowing in the wind, not tied down in case some adjustments have to be made. Numerous

embarrassed predictions from the doomsday prophets of the new millennium (Y-2K) bear eloquent testimony. It is safer to avoid the scrupulous analysis of people who know better. But the biblical writers had no such reluctance. They stood firm on their words and God proved them right. The theological issue of 'lost property' is no small problem.

Let us soberly reflect on the serious problems of 'ongoing revelations', the problems of no brakes, blind faith and lost property. Let us remain confident that God has spoken fully in Scripture, and 'nothing at any time is to be added, whether by new revelations of the Spirit, or human traditions'.

## Questions

1. *Given that our Lord is the both 'the revealer and the revealed', what should we learn from his constant appeal to the written word of God? (See Matthew 12:2-6; 19:4; 21:13; 22:29; 26:31; Mark 4:4-11; 7:6; 12:10; Luke 22:37; John 10:34-36.)*

2. *'Moses was adamant that true revelation should never become lost property.' Is that true? (See Deuteronomy 31:9-13, 24-27, & 36-37.)*

3. *What 'revelations' should preachers tell to the church? (See Acts 17:2-3; 18:4-5; 18:28; Romans 15:4; 1 Corinthians 15:1-4; & 1 Timothy 4:13-16.)*

# 11. How big is the Bible?

*Please read: Matthew 22:23-33*

It is not trivial to ask how big is the Bible. That question touches the pulse of a neglected aspect of divine guidance. There is far more to Scripture than the sum total of its words. That's why David says: 'To all perfection I see a limit; but your commands are boundless. Oh, how I love your law! I meditate on it all day long' (Psalm 119:96-97). To meditate deeply upon Scripture is to discover a sense of its boundlessness. The Bible has logical implications for the myriad paths of life. There is no measurable limit to the guidance it provides.

The problem is that not everyone who believes the Bible appreciates its full extent. That is why they are open to claims of ongoing revelation. The Bible is sufficient to equip us for every good work (2 Timothy 3:16-17). God has spoken fully, giving his people a rich abundance of guidance. But what does this mean? Just how big is the Bible? A correct answer is critical for a proper view of divine guidance. The question asks 'how big' in two senses, namely *the whole canon* and *the whole counsel*.

The first sense refers to how big the Bible is in terms of its authenticity. How many books are genuinely God-breathed 'scripture'? How was the total of sixty-six books decided as the 'whole canon' (measure) of the Bible, and why? The second sense refers to the size of the Bible in terms of its scope. Is the scope of Scripture limited to its actual subject matter? Must the Bible explicitly refer to an issue before it can command our conscience? Do we need a clear 'proof text' commanding a certain duty before we can say God requires it? What is the 'whole counsel' of God? We need to get both of these concepts right, the canon and the counsel.

## The whole canon

The word *canon* means rule, standard, or list. The biblical canon is the list of books recognized as authentic Scripture. What rule or standard led the church to accept sixty-six books in the Bible, no more and no less? The *Westminster Confession* declares:

> The books commonly called Apocrypha, not being of divine inspiration, are no part of the canon of the Scripture. Therefore they have no authority in the Church of God, and are to be treated like any other merely human writings.

How did this become the Christian position? Several matters should be kept in mind.

132

## a. An important distinction

There is a distinction between 'authority' and 'canon'. A book's authority is the most important issue. The only legitimate reason for a book to be in the biblical list (canon) is its inherent divine authority. No book has authority *because* the church canonized it. On the contrary, the church was obliged to list books as canonical because their divine authority was beyond dispute.

A distortion, taught in some secular history courses, alleges the church decided what should be in the Bible and what should not. What really happened is illustrated by what botanists do when drawing up a list of plants belonging to a certain species. Take the 'fern' species, for example. First, these scientists agree on the characteristics and essential qualities of a true fern. Then, any plants with those qualities are added to the list (canon) of ferns. Likewise, the Christian church first agreed on the qualities belonging to true Scripture. Then, since exactly sixty-six books of that sort have been found, only those sixty-six books constitute the canon (list) of Scripture.

The church was simply recognizing what God had done. The authority (quality) of each inspired book was already in it. The church did not impart that authority, but simply recognized it, and was obliged to list it for that reason. Likewise with the ferns, the scientists did not give plants their special *fern* qualities. They simply recognized those inherent qualities and were obliged to list them.

## b. The need for a list

The need for a decision about the canon arose because of inevitable claims and questions regarding books other than the sixty-six in our Bible. For example, the first few verses in Luke's Gospel mention various other written accounts about Jesus. Why are these other 'gospel' records not included in the canon with Luke's account? Various books are also favourably cited in the Old Testament, but are not regarded as 'Scripture'. They include *The Book of Jashar* (Joshua 10:13), *The Book of the Wars of The Lord* (Numbers 21:14), and *The Chronicles/ Annals of the Kings of Israel* (2 Chronicles 33:18). Whatever superb qualities they undoubtedly had, they are not part of the authentic inspired word of God.

Other problems confronted the church. Some rabbis questioned the book of Esther because it does not contain the name of God. There were also translation problems. Long before Christ, versions of Scripture representing wrong canonical views began to emerge. The church could not stand by in silence. A good example is *The Samaritan Pentateuch,* containing only the first five books of the Old Testament. Samaritans rejected all the other Hebrew Scriptures (the writings and the Prophets).

In the middle of the second century a heretic named Marcion issued his own canon, rejecting over half the New Testament books. He accepted only eleven books, namely Luke's Gospel and only ten of Paul's thirteen letters. Even Marcion's version of Luke was significantly abridged because he lopped off any parts that he considered were 'too Jewish'.

Another problem was that of Montanism (the second-century charismatic movement). It represented the opposite extreme to Marcion's truncated canon. Montanus wanted an open canon. He claimed that God was still speaking words of revelation, especially through him! He made grandiose claims, even calling himself the promised 'Paraclete' (divine helper). He and his followers claimed to be prophets, thus creating an élitist group within the church. They rejected the notion of a closed canon, that God had spoken his final word in the New Testament books.

## c. The process

Arriving at the list of sixty-six books was a process over time, in which all claims were carefully investigated and debated. There was never any real question about the Old Testament, since Jesus and the Apostles used the Hebrew canon of thirty-seven books. The main debates concerned the New Testament.

Considering that the last book of the Bible was not written until about A.D. 96, it is encouraging to see how quickly substantial agreement was reached. The earliest Christian writers, the 'apostolic fathers' (A.D. 100-140), recognized and accepted the four Gospels and the collected letters of Paul as fully authoritative. They appealed with finality to texts from each of the four Gospels, and to passages from Paul. Most of the Pauline letters are quoted. They refer explicitly to 'the four Gospels', and to 'Paul's letters'. They had received these books as *collections* bearing final authority in the church. These collections comprise 70% of the New Testament. By A.D. 140 at least 70% of the New Testament was already operating as authoritative scripture. Eighty years later 91% of the New Testament was operating, without dispute, as fully authoritative within the whole church.

Which books were disputed? They were mainly those for which some doubts had been raised about apostolic authorship.

Some disputed Hebrews, James, 2 Peter, and 2-3 John because they could not find their predecessors in the church citing these books as Scripture. Jude and Revelation were disputed, primarily by Bishop Eusebius early in the fourth century, but he was not upheld in his dissent. Some other disputed books eventually lost support even from those who once promoted them, three examples being:

- *The Shepherd of Hermas*, which claimed to be visions from God, but without any connection to the circle of the apostles, and often speculative in content;
- *The Didache*, a list of regulations for church life from Turkey at about A.D. 100;
- *The Revelation of Peter*, which was very similar to the Revelation of John.

These sorts of remaining questions were resolved through a series of church councils in both East and West, which worked toward a full consensus on the matter. The first canonical list identical to our present New Testament (twenty-seven books) was published by Bishop Athanasius of Alexandria in A.D. 367. Part of the famous 'Paschal Letter', this list was widely influential in resolving various smaller debates of the canonical issue. The Synod of Rome, meeting in 382, accepted the Athanasian list. But one more meeting was required.

There needed to be a meeting of both the Eastern bishops and the Western bishops, so that the list would have full, ecumenical authority for all the churches. That was achieved in Carthage, North Africa, in A.D. 397. Christians look to the Synod of Carthage as achieving the final recognition of the full canon of the New Testament. In 419 the Council of Carthage reaffirmed the same decision. How big is the Bible? In terms of size and content, sixty-six books! That has been settled for over fifteen centuries.

## The whole counsel

Now the question needs to be asked in a different sense. How big is the Bible in terms of the scope of its authority? Does the Bible have to explicitly speak about something in order to command our conscience? Is a clear 'proof text' needed? In what way does Scripture express God's counsel (his mind and will) for us? Just how extensive is the 'guidance' Scripture provides?

This is answered in the *Westminster Confession of Faith*, 1:6:

> The whole counsel of God, concerning all things necessary for His own glory, man's salvation, faith and life, is either expressly stated in Scripture, or by good and necessary reasoning may be deduced from Scripture: nothing at any time is to be added, whether by new revelations of the Spirit, or human traditions.

The Bible is big enough to provide 'the *whole* counsel of God' not just some of it. It does not need supplementing or updating. It is never inadequate or out of date. It provides everything we need to know in order to glorify God acceptably. It provides everything we need to know about salvation, and about what to believe ('faith'), and about how to live. Nothing is missing from this divine guidance. The Bible provides it all. But the Bible is bigger than the mathematical summation of its words! All proper deductions flowing from the written text are binding upon us. It is essential to notice the function of logical reasoning.

*The human mind matters!* True Christianity insists on logical reasoning. There is a true sense of 'primacy of the intellect'. We are to love God 'with our whole mind'. We are not only to read and believe Scripture, but also to 'meditate on it day and night', engaging in rigorous thought about it. This meditation develops a full and rich theology, as it chases the explicit statements of Scripture right through to their valid implications.

As Paul shows in Romans 1:20, this duty of making logical deductions applies not only to special revelation (Scripture) but also to general revelation (creation). 'For since the creation of the world God's invisible qualities — his eternal power and divine nature — have been clearly seen, being understood from what has been made, so that men are without excuse.' As a revelation to the naked eye, the creation conveys serious consequences (implications) to the mind and conscience of every man. From observing creation, every man *can* deduce what God is like, and *should* deduce those truths about God, and is held *accountable* to do

> We are not only to read and believe Scripture, but also to *'meditate on it day and night'*, engaging in rigorous thought about it.

so. There is no excuse for failure. There is no atheism. There is only suppression of the truth in unrighteousness. There is only a refusal to acknowledge the God who is known.

A prime example concerns the probationary command in Eden. From God's explicit command about the forbidden tree, Adam and Eve were bound to make logical deductions. Those deductions carry the same authority as the words God actually spoke. Thus they immediately knew that there was such a thing as *evil* (though it was not something God created or that they had experienced). Also the meaning of *death* (unknown in Eden and not defined in the command) was logically inferred by the command itself. A whole string of inferences were implied about the nature of God and man. It was obvious that God judges men and holds them fully accountable. It was also clear that human innocence could be lost and immortality was conditional on obedience. So Adam already had chapters ready for an original edition of *Systematic Theology*, chapters on the doctrine of God and the doctrine of man.

The unwritten implications of the Bible are just as much 'God's will' as the written words! Adding the two together (what is written and what is implied) gives us 'the whole counsel of God', the whole of God's guidance for us. Christianity demands good scholarship, nothing but the very best! It is sad to see the simplistic naiveté in parts of the Christian church today. There is an unmistakable anti-intellectual ethos that demands 'chapter and verse' before any statement is accepted: it is not surprising that this 'no verse, no case' attitude to divine guidance provides an open door for fresh supplies of revelation. When the authority of the Bible is reduced to mere literalism, there can be no such thing as the sufficiency of Scripture.

In his famous 'Sermon on the Mount' Jesus opposed the Pharisees for such a reductionist mentality. They knew the law explicitly forbade murder but they ignored its logical implications. As long as they didn't literally murder anyone they presumed murderous thoughts, desires and words were legitimate. Jesus exposed this narrow distorted way of misusing Scripture. He showed how the same law that *explicitly* forbids adultery also *implicitly* forbids all sexual immorality and lust.

A great deal of Christian doctrine is not taught explicitly in Scripture, but is derived by proper reasoning from it (like the doctrine of the Trinity). Jesus showed the binding nature of logical implications by using that method himself. When Sadducees denied the resurrection, Jesus said: *'Have you not read what God said to you*, "I am the God of Abraham, the God of Isaac, and the God of Jacob"? He is not the God of the dead but of the living' (Matthew 22:31-32). By plain logic, if Abraham (who died) belongs to God, but God is not the God of the dead, then Abraham still truly lives (there must be a resurrection)!

The same logic is evident in the preaching of the Apostles. Over and over again they 'reasoned from the Scriptures that Jesus was the Christ', which means they drew out the reasonable implications from what was explicitly written (Acts 18:4-5). There is no Old Testament verse saying in black and white that 'Jesus of Nazareth is the true Messiah', but that is clearly the implication of the whole.

As a mundane example, we can say the Bible requires Australians to drive on the left-hand side of the road. That is the logical implication from texts requiring obedience to the governing authorities and concern for the safety of neighbours.

If a person in Australia drives on the other side, it is not only unlawful, it is actually unbiblical.

How big is the Bible? It is very big, far bigger than the total of its pages. It includes every logical conclusion implied by the written words. Let us be done with all small views of the Bible. It is a vast treasure. And let us have a great dislike for *biblicist* methods (simplistic and reductionist misuses). Let these facts edify and equip us. Praise God for everything Scripture says and implies. Praise God for his totally sufficient guidance in the Bible.

## Questions

1. *'In parables especially, God's will is found in the logical implications rather than the actual words.' Assess that comment using Matthew 13:44-46.*

2. *In John 10:31-36 Jesus defends his deity by appealing to the 'good and necessary consequences' (logical inferences) arising from Psalm 82:6. What are these logical inferences, and how do they silence his critics?*

3. *The implications of Christ's words in Nazareth made the people angry enough to kill him. What did they see implied, and were they correct (Luke 4:16-30)?*

# 12. Interpreting divine guidance

*Please read: 2 Peter 3*

Even the best guidance can lead to disaster if it is wrongly interpreted. Most of us have experienced this. If we are in unfamiliar territory we ask a 'local' for directions. Even if he gives us accurate guidance, we can still go wrong by misunderstanding something he said. The same is true of divine guidance. It is certainly accurate, but we need to interpret it correctly. Humans can misunderstand both the explicit teachings and the logical implications of the Bible. When right guidance is wrongly interpreted, foolish decisions occur. Worse, the act of committing a serious mistake is comforted by the delusional thought of obeying God! One word describes the key issue here … *hermeneutics*.

*Hermeneutics* means *interpretation* and the *principles of interpreting*. Without even thinking about it we are doing hermeneutics all the time. It is as natural as breathing and just as important and unobtrusive. Every moment of the day we are interpreting the things around us. We cannot read a newspaper, have a conversation, watch a movie, or cross the road without doing hermeneutics, interpreting things.

Even as you read these words, your mind is applying interpretive principles so that you can 'get my drift'. Those last three words illustrate your hermeneutics. You didn't take them literally. You know that I'm not actually drifting anywhere. You know what 'get my drift' means. It means you'll 'cotton on'. And that is not a reference to literal cotton, though I think you follow my 'thread' (without *woolly thinking*).

We learn the basic rules of interpretation without ever formally studying them. We soak them up from our culture as we grow. Every one of us has a very sophisticated programme of hermeneutical skills in our minds, acting as a grid through which we sieve every single idea, word and message. It goes in as raw data (just plain literal words, for instance) but it comes out as an understood message. Quite often our correct understanding (interpretation) bears no resemblance to the literal words in the raw data.

For example, if someone complains, 'He let the cat out of the bag,' we do not think of an animal gaining its freedom. When we read, 'The customer is always right', we know the shop doesn't think we are infallible. When teenagers say something is 'cool' it probably has nothing to do with temperature. The answer to 'How are you going?' may be 'Very well thanks,' or 'By taxi', depending on the context quickly assessed by the mind. To say 'She broke down' might refer to a car stopping unexpectedly, or it might mean a distressed woman. It is all a matter of hermeneutics.

When it comes to interpreting the Bible, the same hermeneutical processes apply, with some additional ones arising because it is the infallible word of God. But we cannot assume that these proper principles of biblical interpretation will come naturally. They don't, and this is why Christians with the same high view of the Bible can come to very different conclusions. So what is involved? What are the rules for safe interpretation of God's Word? It is a large subject, but two key principles deserve our attention now:

1.  The principle of true harmony
2.  The principle of true scholarship

## The principle of true harmony

God is infinite in wisdom, knowledge, rationality and reliability. What he teaches us in one part of Scripture cannot contradict what he says in another part. Every part of God's guidance is in harmony with the whole of it. This is sometimes called 'the analogy of faith'. It is the most basic starting point. If a person does not accept that, there is no real point reading the Bible. It is well stated in the *Westminster Confession* 1:9:

> The infallible rule for the interpretation of the Bible is the Bible itself. Therefore, when there is a question about the true and full meaning of any passage in the Bible (which is a consistent unity), it must be searched and known by other passages that speak more clearly.

We will look at several issues here.

145

## a. No contradiction

To assume the Bible can contradict itself, and that it needs to be corrected by other more reliable sources, is proof of an unregenerate mind.[1] The very suggestion that God could speak incorrectly, or speak from ignorance, or contradict himself, is blasphemy. It is proof that a person is bereft of the Holy Spirit.

So we are committed to the rational integrity of Scripture. Every small part of it accords perfectly with the entire product. When we interpret any part of the Bible (a verse, a paragraph, a whole book) it cannot contradict any other part. If there is a contradiction, our interpretation is certainly wrong. So we are committed to looking at the 'bigger picture'.

A helpful illustration of this can be taken from the production of a movie. A movie film is a long line of single frames projected sequentially at high speed. The one 'big picture' is made up of many 'small pictures'. We are not entitled to interpret any single scene (frame) in a way that is later disproved by some other frames or by the movie as a whole. Producers often try to trick the audience into doing exactly that, coming to a premature judgement. That's part of the appeal of the 'whodunits'. They induce us to interpret the early evidence wrongly. But that evidence takes on a new meaning when a clever twist is

> When we interpret any part of the Bible (a verse, a paragraph, a whole book) it cannot contradict any other part.

introduced later in the story. Interpreting the Bible is analogous. We need to know the full story in order to do justice to any part of it.

## b. No external interpreter

No person or institution is qualified to impose an interpretation of Scripture upon our conscience or to claim that we must consult them because they alone have the infallible interpretation. No one can say, 'The Bible does not speak clearly enough by itself, you must listen to me. You need me to explain what God means.' As the *Westminster Confession* declares: 'The infallible rule for the interpretation of the Bible is the Bible itself.' The Bible is its own interpreter, and while it is good and proper to seek help from people with better knowledge, in the end we must decide if their teaching lines up with Scripture. We must do what the Bereans did when Paul preached: 'they received the message with great eagerness and examined the Scriptures every day, to see if what Paul said was true' (Acts 17:11).

All sorts of dangerous groups deny this important principle. Rationalists make human reason the infallible rule of interpretation, so they will not accept anything that human reason cannot understand. That leads to denying the existence of God and miracles. The Roman Catholic Church emphatically denies this principle. 'The Church is the perfectly trustworthy guide and teacher ... that sense (of Scripture) which has been and is held by our Holy Mother the church ... is the judgement of the true sense and interpretation of the Holy Scriptures, so that nobody is allowed to explain Holy Scripture contrary to that sense or the unanimous opinion of the Fathers.'[2] Under that system it is unnecessary for individuals to read the Bible. All they have to do is believe whatever the church says.

Precisely the same is true of the Watchtower Society. The founder, Charles Russell, published his own private interpretations under the title of 'Scripture Studies', and then said that the Bible itself was unnecessary!

> Not only do we find that people cannot see the divine plan in studying the Bible by itself, but we see, also, that if anyone lays the 'Scripture Studies' aside, even after he has used them ... after he has read them for ten years, if he then lays them aside and ignores them and goes to the Bible alone, though he has understood his Bible for ten years, our experience shows that within two years he goes into darkness. On the other hand, if he had merely read the 'Scripture Studies' with their references and had not read a page of the Bible as such, he would be in the light at the end of two years, because he would have the light of the Scriptures.[3]

Such religious bondage and manipulation gives us good reason to rejoice in the liberty of orthodox Christianity! We are free to judge all human interpretations by Scripture alone. 'The infallible rule for the interpretation of the Bible is the Bible itself.'

## c. No hidden meaning

In every age foolish people have treated Scripture as a wax nose, bending and shaping it as they please. Essentially they deny that Scripture is true literature, to be interpreted by the normal rules of grammar, context and literary genre (recognizing the differences between poetry and narrative, parable and prophecy). Instead they impose artificial schemes to search for hidden meanings behind the printed words. A recent example of this is *The Bible Code*, which claims the Bible carries secret messages about Shakespeare's plays, the Oklahoma bomber, the invention of the light bulb, the Wright brothers, Winston Churchill and Albert Einstein.[4] (See more details in the next chapter.)

In the second and third centuries Origen found hidden meanings by allegorizing the Bible, a habit that was rife by the Middle Ages. Thus Rahab's scarlet cord meant the blood of Christ, Abraham's three visitors meant the Trinity, the six stone water pots used in Christ's first miracle are the six days of creation. Christians can and do make the mistake in other ways. Common problems include twisted forms of *Christocentricity* (looking for Christ in every text) or resorting to *moralism* (reducing every event or character to a moral lesson).

It needs to be clearly understood that the text of Scripture has one meaning, namely that meaning required by the context (the grammatical, historical and literary context). There are no hidden meanings, no higher and lower meanings, no 'deeper senses', and no mystical messages to be dredged up from beneath the surface of the words. None of this denies that texts may have a richer outworking than the bare words convey. To illustrate, consider the first statement of the gospel, the seed of the woman promised in Genesis 3:15. Here God describes a male child who will take sides with man against the serpent, successfully defending man against the tempter, crushing his head. But it involves pain and injury for the saviour (a bruised heel). That is what the text originally meant, still means and always will mean.

However, the precise way in which the details unravel is taught in other, later texts. Who is this promised son? When will he come? How will he do this saving work? What will the extent of his injury be (being struck on the heel)? These details do not belong to that first gospel text and they should not be forced into it from hindsight. The meaning of any text is found in its own historical, grammatical and linguistic context. That meaning never changes though it may be the first in an unfolding string of texts progressively telling more and more detail. God is not saying to the audience in Genesis 3: 'I'll send Jesus of Nazareth, my Son, born of the Virgin Mary, to die on a Roman cross in order to save men from the snare of the devil.' To put that interpretation on his words is to violate every basic principle of good interpretation. It is to impose hidden meanings onto the text.


## The principle of true scholarship

Nothing is more likely to harm the church and multiply errors than entrusting her pulpits to people untrained and ungifted for explaining the Word of God. There is a need for competent scholarship in rightly dividing the word of truth. The *Westminster Confession* recognizes this (1:7):

> The meanings of all things in Scripture are not equally plain in themselves, or equally clear to all people. However, those things which it is necessary to know,

believe, and do, regarding salvation, are so clearly stated and explained in one part of Scripture or another, that the untrained person as well as the scholar can sufficiently understand them by a proper use of the ordinary means.

On one hand, an untrained person, properly using the ordinary means of interpretation, is quite capable of understanding the key teachings of Scripture regarding sin and salvation. It requires no genius to understand 'None is righteous not even one', or 'Believe on the Lord Jesus Christ and you shall be saved.' Ordinary people can understand such things using ordinary abilities. On the other hand...

*a. Some things are hard to interpret*

Not all things in the Bible are so straightforward. They are 'not equally plain in themselves, or equally clear to all people'. The Bible contains 'some things hard to understand, which ignorant and unstable people distort, as they do the other Scriptures, to their own destruction' (2 Peter 3:16). So we recognize the danger of ignorance in biblical interpretation. We are committed to good scholarship.

*b. Some people know more*

The ultimate authority of Scripture is located in the original Hebrew and Greek writings. Therefore every dispute about what the Bible means has to be settled by appealing to these original languages. So we depend on people who are competent in the use of those languages. They are key witnesses in the final court of appeal. But we recognize that most people are not scholars. It would not be good if they were. The body is made up of various parts having different gifts. We confess that 'Because these original tongues are not known to all the people of God, who have a right to the Scriptures, and are commanded, in the fear of God, to read and search them, therefore they are to be translated into the common language of every nation' (WCF 1:8).

We must not neglect this distinction. We must not ignore good scholarship. We all depend on it. Even the best scholars depend on other scholars. No man is an island. But there is a rampant individualism abroad today that is very dangerous. It exaggerates the equality of all believers. It assumes that any man's opinion about the meaning of a text is as credible as the next man's opinion, deserving equal exposure for discussion. It assumes that the opinion of a babe in Christ has as much value as the opinion of a genius like John Calvin or a colossus like the Westminster Assembly. But this is certainly not the case.

The proof is self-evident. While a new Christian has sufficiently understood the need to repent, will he also be made Professor of Systematic Theology? Will a man converted this morning write Bible commentaries tonight? Of course not. We all implicitly recognize that competent knowledge has various degrees. Scripture makes this point very clear: 'Do not think of yourself more highly than you ought, but rather think of yourself with sober judgement, in accordance with the measure of faith God has given you' (Romans 12:3).

## c. Some examples

Proper interpretation of Scripture means commitment to good scholarship, especially regarding the grammar, context and

**152**

literature. The Bible is a large collection of literary works. Like other libraries the Bible contains an amazing diversity. There is a variety of genre (forms) such as historical narrative, law, poetry, proverbial wisdom literature, prophetic discourse, epistles, parable, hyperbole and apocalyptic. Failure to recognize the implications of this causes lots of problems. Different literature has different ways of using words and ideas to convey a message. The rules for interpreting poetry are not the same as for narrative. Joel's prophecy is not to be read like Paul's letters. We cannot simply put all texts on a dead-level plain and take them 'literally' in their plain straightforward sense. Just think what nonsense would emerge from a literal interpretation of Christ's words, 'I am the vine, you are the branches.'

What does literalism do with Isaiah's words, 'The mountains and the hills will break forth into *shouts* of joy before you, and all the trees of the field will *clap* their hands' (Isaiah 55:12, NASB)? What about the psalmist's words: 'The nations made an uproar, the kingdoms tottered; He raised His voice, the earth *melted*' (Psalm 46:6, NASB)? When Paul tells us that during the Exodus at the Red Sea, God's people 'drank from the spiritual rock that accompanied them, and that rock was Christ' (1 Corinthians 10:4, NIV), what nonsense we get from interpreting it literally according to the 'plain straightforward sense of the words'.

There is a problem with the gimmicky mantra, 'God said it, I believe it, that settles it.' The implication is that the Word of God is transparently simple, requiring no intense thought about its meaning. It seems that merely quoting what God said instantly settles the question of what he meant by it.

It is not uncommon for preachers to be asked, 'Do you believe the Bible literally?' What is the appropriate answer? It should be along the following lines. No, I only take the Bible literally where the grammar and context require it, but I take it poetically, or figuratively, or thematically, or symbolically, or proverbially where the grammar and context require it. I do not believe the sun literally sets or that Jesus is a literal grape vine or that the trees have literal hands to clap.

Let us never forget the wise old maxim: 'A text without its context is a pretext!' May God make us wise and thoughtful interpreters of his word. Let us be committed to true harmony and true scholarship. A wise man values the historic creeds. A wise man stays in the main stream of orthodox scholarship. To interpret divine guidance (Scripture) in novel ways, foreign to the church of all ages, is a recipe for disaster. Let us be determined to handle Scripture accurately.

## Questions

1. *What principles of good interpretation are identified or implied in 2 Peter 3 and Matthew 24:42-51?*

2. *What problems would arise from a literalist interpretation of Revelation 1:9-11?*

3. *'Interpreting a text in its context does not preclude validly applying it to another context.' Comment on that in the light of Psalm 95 and Hebrews 3:7-19.*

# 13. Guidance gone mad

## The 'Bible Code' folly

*Please read: 1 Timothy 1:1-11*

The teaching of mythical nonsense in the church is nothing new. Back in A.D. 63, the apostle Paul told Timothy to put an end to it. 'Command certain men not to teach false doctrines any longer nor to devote themselves to myths and endless genealogies' (1 Timothy 1:3-4). In every age there has been a ready supply of Christian 'guidance' from blind guides who 'do not know what they are talking about or what they so confidently affirm' (1 Timothy 1:7).

An example is the alleged 'Bible Code'. The first version (Mark I) appeared in 1997 when the agnostic journalist Michael Drosnin published his book *The Bible Code*. A new version (Mark II) of the same theory came in a book written by Larry Mitcham, entitled *September 11 is in the Bible Code* (Pacific International University, 2001).

According to Mitcham, what you see in your normal Bible is called 'the surface text' (pp. 12 and 103) or 'the plain text'

(p. 54), below which is a secret agenda hidden in 'code'. The whole thing is a highly arbitrary, speculative and subjective deviation from Christian orthodoxy. It is a computer-generated word game of no more use to Christian maturity than anything Nintendo puts out. What follows now is an assessment of both versions of the 'Bible Code': Bible Code Mark I and Bible Code Mark II.

## Bible Code Mark I

In 1984 Michael Drosnin read an article published in a maths journal and it went to his head. It was about *Equidistant Lettering Sequences* (ELSs). He claims that by observing them using computers, he discovered coded (hidden) prophecies predicting lots of recent twentieth-century events, including the assassination of Israeli Prime Minister Yitzak Rabin. These 'messages' exist in randomly grouped Hebrew letters, sometimes across the page, sometimes down, sometimes diagonally, sometimes forwards and sometimes backwards. In other words, there is an artificial manipulation of the printed text to find names, which are then assumed to be 'messages'.

The book makes ludicrous claims about the Bible. For instance, 'We have always thought of the Bible as a book... It is also a computer program' (p. 45). It claims that all of history is written in the Bible: 'All that was, is, and will be unto the end of time is included in the Torah' (p. 44). This is not hyperbolic but is meant in the fullest literal sense. It points out the encoded predictions of Shakespeare's plays, the name of the Oklahoma bomber, the invention of the light bulb, the Wright brothers, Winston Churchill, Einstein and gravity.

## Bible Code Mark II

Though Larry Mitcham uses exactly the same technique as Drosnin, he makes conscious efforts to claim more credibility. He distances himself from some of Drosnin's applications of the 'code', and he wants readers to treat the actual Bible text, the 'surface text', seriously. His rule is: 'Make sure that any "new" material agrees with doctrines already known in the "uncoded" Bible' (p. 57). But all of this reassurance is irrelevant. Nothing changes the fact that the Bible Code is artificial, mythical and mere imagination.

Mitcham's 'rule' is incredulous given the ridiculous claims in the book. For instance, he claims that numerous personal and professional details of Clifford Wilson[1] are in the Bible. This includes the name of his deceased first wife (Avis), his four children (Bruce, Elaine, David & Lynette), his father (William Lucas Wilson), his mother's name (Isabelle), the place of his birth (Sydney, Australia), the full maiden name of his second wife (Barbara Joan Baddeley), her date of birth and other personal details (see p. 35).

This is entirely subjective. How does Mitcham know 'Avis' doesn't refer to the Car Rental Company? Are there no other people called Bruce, or Elaine, or David? Did nothing else happen in Sydney, Australia, except the birth of Clifford Wilson? How can anyone take this seriously? Moreover, none of these names occur as 'words' (where the letters immediately follow each other, like **S-y-d-n-e-y**). They are only there if you take one letter from one word on a page and the next letter from another word (maybe not even on that page or even in that biblical book) then the next letter from some other word in some other place. And then you 'join' them up in any direction to form the name.

The chance of finding 'words' like that depends entirely on the value you set for the ELSs ('skip intervals'). Mitcham himself says: 'With the Bible Code, you put a word into the computer and you are given a particular skip sequence which could be as low as one or as high as thousands' (p. 83). If you set it at zero (skipping no letters) you have no chance of finding anything except the actual words in the Bible. But as you increase it from one to thousands you increase the chance of finding the bits and pieces you desire. But that is simply a game of mathematical chance. A bigger field gives a bigger chance. The Bible is made to resemble a giant wrecking yard for someone wanting to build a car out of bits and pieces. The more wrecks you have, the better your chance of finding all the bits and pieces: a wheel here, a gearbox there, and a seat somewhere else. The size of the wrecking yard (ELS) is entirely arbitrary: pick any number you like and see what results! Some examples will clarify.

*'Words' allegedly found*

Mitcham claims to have found the following coded words regarding the events in America in late 2001: *Anthrax, world, trade, centre, skyjacked, terror, fireman, Afghan, September 11, President, George, Bush, Osama, Bin, Laden, New, York, smallpox, Taliban.* But the letters for those words are all over the place, from Psalms and Proverbs all the way into Malachi! The 'skip intervals' vary from plus 16,556 to minus 16,549 (*plus* means reading forward from a certain point, *minus* means reading backwards).

Consider what it says about 'New York': 'Psalm 72 verse 10 gives us the starting point for the word 'New', and Psalm 68 verse 13 being the starting point for the word 'York' ' (p. 110). There are 97 verses between these two points, 97 verses between the letter 'N' (allegedly N for 'New') and the letter 'Y' (allegedly Y for 'York') and that's reading backwards! What sort of anti-intellectual folly is this? And who says that 'New' is linked to 'York'? If even their first letters are 97 verses apart, what sort of 'rule' is being applied here? Why couldn't it be 'New Avis', or 'New President' or 'New Bin'? Why couldn't the York refer to York Street, Sydney, or the English city of York? All these words are allegedly in the code.

Even if we granted the argument that these coded words are for real, they are not *teaching* anything. There are no logical connections between them. They do not form sentences. They make no propositions. They are not statements, or warnings, or declarations, or exhortations, or questions, or prophecies, or interpretations. They are, at best, just bare jumbled words! Any 'meaning' is what the reader himself imposes! A thousand different readers could impose a thousand different 'meanings'. It is no different to watching the game of scrabble. Lots of unrelated words progressively appear on the board in all directions. Only a fool would build them into a message!

*What is this?*

Apart from anything else, this is an utter abuse of the Hebrew language. The code is a magic wand producing rabbits out of a hat. It produces concepts totally foreign to the Hebrew culture of the biblical writers. It is madness to allege that David and Moses and Malachi actually wrote coded messages about New York City or Sydney or Clifford Wilson. Those writers had no idea of Afghan or anthrax, of skyjacked aircraft (or any other sort of aircraft). It is no good trying to avoid that criticism, saying it is the wonderful inspirational nature of Scripture. It is a false view of the doctrine of inspiration that bypasses the mind of the human writers.[2] It turns Scripture into a game of chance and pure mythology. You may as well search for Mickey Mouse and the Loch Ness monster. They will be there in the code if you choose the right lettering sequences.

*The wedding party*

The utterly manipulative and arbitrary nature of the 'code' is highlighted in the example described on pages 40-42. Mitcham's friend, Rev. Ron Jenkins, had a daughter about to be married. Was this wedding in the Bible? Was her name and that of her husband in Scripture? They thought it would be a nice wedding gift for them if they could show them such a marvellous thing. So Mitcham says, 'I booted up our largest computer, and I was frustrated to find that after three days I still had no results.' Did he call it quits? No. Did he eventually get the results he wanted? Yes. What trustworthy, credible, orthodox hermeneutic did he use?

> Then I had a bright idea. I called Dr. Baugh (another friend of the wedding party) and I asked him to have his daughter email me a copy of her wedding invitation ... the invitation arrived and it contained a list of all

her family members, the list of all the bridesmaids, the children, and even the grandparents. I used a special software that is designed for searching for large numbers of words in a cluster at one time, and as a result I quickly found the anchor page. Then I began to look for each separate name on that list, and to my surprise, every one was there. We are talking about a list of over 120 words, names, dates, places and events — and, I repeat, they were all there. The bridegroom's last name was 'Barney', so we have called the page the Barney-Jenkins Page.[3]

How arbitrary can one get? If the code doesn't work, wrack your brains for some bright idea to make it work! But why use details from her wedding invitation? Why not use her passport, or driver's licence, or credit card, or the key words in her last college assignment? This is a prime application of the 'myths', the 'meaningless talk', and playing with words or 'endless genealogies' forbidden by Paul. It degrades Christianity. There are no controls here. This is just a mindless subjective game of 'find the hidden words'.

*Am I in the code?*

By now you may be wondering who else has their personal genealogical and professional details encoded in the Bible. On page 39 the question is asked for you, the reader: 'Am I in the Bible Code?' The answer is yes! Indeed, the book postulates that everything about everybody is hidden in the Bible Code! 'It would seem extremely likely that … all the history of the world and its occupants is in the hidden resources of God's Word. What an astounding possibility!' (p. 42).

Clearly Mitcham cannot distance himself from Drosnin because he essentially agrees with his comment: 'All that was, is, and will be unto the end of time is included in the Torah.' This is an entirely wrong view of Scripture. The Bible is not a book about 'everything'. It is a book about God's plan of salvation. Scripture is 'salvation history', not 'all history'. The Bible is selective not comprehensive. The Bible is all about God's covenant plan, covenant people and covenant achievements. It does not enhance Scripture to claim it as a comprehensive record of every microscopic detail in the universe. That actually debases the Bible. It loses sight of its Christological focus. Mythology is bad enough, but when it becomes 'baptized mythology' in the church we have serious trouble. This reinforces why it is very important for Christians to stay in step with the historic faith of the church expressed in her great creeds.

> The Bible is not a book about 'everything'. It is a book about God's plan of salvation.

Thankfully, some stinging criticisms of the 'Bible Code' have been published. One of them is very aptly named *Snake Oil For sale* (by Shlomo Sternberg, *Bible Review*, August 1997). Sternberg pointed out that if you apply the same code to *Moby Dick* similar results occur. Mitcham is aware of this and does not dispute it. His response is: 'This does not rule out a different kind of "code" as a possible literary tool used by the Holy Spirit of God in compiling Scripture' (p. 25). This is blind, irrational and incredulous. How convenient to say 'that's different' when the evidence torpedoes your theory!

Several conclusions are unavoidable. First, from a purely mathematical point of view, the whole thing is arbitrary and contrived. Lettering sequences occur in every piece of extended writing, including the telephone directory! They turn meaningful literature into a mere pool of alphabetical symbols (like those used for the board game 'Scrabble'). Who decides the 'equidistance' between letters? Working with a language like Hebrew (with huge numbers of tri-consonant word roots and originally having no vowels) it is not hard to discover a random combination forming a 'word' (message). But is that any more rational than reading tealeaves in a cup?

Secondly, since the Bible is treated as a pool of letters, true exegesis is abolished. True exegesis interprets by means of grammar, literary genre and context. None of these are relevant with a 'Bible Code'. Who cares anymore about the historic setting of a book, or the author, or the audience? Who cares about the verbal tenses (past, present, or future), or the verbal voices (active or passive), or the verbal moods (indicative, imperative, or infinitive)? Who cares whether the words are nouns, prepositions, definite articles or participles? Who cares that they are even coherent words? So long as they are just letters shaken out on a page, there is a 'coded message' for anyone determined to find one. This is the death of literature!

Thirdly, Jesus never treated Scripture like that. He always referred to the written text. His constant cry was 'It is written' but never 'It is encoded'. The Apostles did the same. They always preached and explained the written text. They had no such silly ideas as the 'surface text' with layers of 'encoded texts' below it. They interpreted Scripture grammatically, contextually and linguistically. They treated proverbs as proverbs and poetry as poetry and historical narrative as literal fact. They showed how it all connected to Christ. The Bible Code is a novelty, an error, and a foolish myth.

Perhaps a light-hearted illustration will help. Suppose I make this confession: 'The words I have written in this book do not convey my real message. They merely form my "surface text". What I really want to say is secretly encoded. Now it is up to you to decode it.' Naturally, this would leave you feeling annoyed and deceived. You assumed everything was literally genuine, but that code-agenda ruins credibility and trust. Of course the confession is merely tongue-in-cheek ... but what if it depicted reality?

## Questions

1. *'Every word of God is flawless; he is a shield to those who take refuge in him. Do not add to his words, or he will rebuke you and prove you a liar' (Proverbs 30:5-6). How does this help us to assess claims of 'coded' Bible messages? (Also see Deuteronomy 4:2 & 12:32.)*

2. *From the following texts, what is the evidence that nothing of the intended message was hidden beneath the words written? (See Luke 1:1-4; 1 Timothy 1:3-11; Titus 1:5-16; & Galatians 6:11.)*

# 14. Beyond mere legitimacy

*Please read: Romans 14*

G ood decision-making is often more complex than simply acting according to biblical freedom. In order to honour God we need to move beyond mere legitimacy. Even when we are certain that a course of action is valid in itself, a good decision does not end there. Other factors may have to be considered. That seems to be the point made by the apostle Paul: '"Everything is permissible for me" — but not everything is beneficial. "Everything is permissible for me" — but I will not be mastered by anything' (1 Corinthians 6:12). Not even our God-given freedom can act as the last court of appeal.

Three examples will help to clarify the complexities, namely, decisions connected with scruples, marriage and gospel ministry.

## Decisions and scruples

In Romans 14 Paul deals with Christians who are too sensitive ('weaker brothers'). They have needless scruples of conscience in matters of no consequence. They do not realize that their mental reservations are about non-gospel issues, things that are religiously and morally neutral. Immature Christians make a 'big deal' out of such things. They make rules: *You shall not eat this, you shall not drink that, and you shall not go there.* The weaker brother puts 'keep off the grass' signs where God says we are free to walk. This has to be considered in the decisions made by others.

'It is better not to eat meat or drink wine or to do anything else that will cause your brother to fall' (Romans 14:21). We have an obligation to avoid giving offence regarding the known scruples of known brothers in known company. However, this should not be exaggerated. Paul is not referring to unknown scruples, as if we should never exercise our freedom because there is always some chance that a weaker brother will see it and be offended. It would be wrong to serve meat to a brother if I know he has scruples about meat. But beyond that I am free. The Bible does not endorse the paranoia of always expecting the worst-case scenario. We are not to constantly wonder whether a weak brother may be watching us. The blood of Christ won our freedoms. They are not to be marginalized by the fear of every possible human scruple. That would deny the very freedoms Paul protects.

The guidance given in Romans 14 cannot be reduced to the simplistic formula that 'If anyone anywhere has a scruple, accommodate it by denying your freedom.' On the contrary, the text deals with the dangers of two-way traffic in matters of liberty and indifference. In one direction it protects weaker brothers against unloving, judgemental and dismissive treatment from stronger Christians. The strong are to accommodate the weak in a gracious way that preserves peace and fellowship. In the other direction it guards against that accommodation going too far. The text makes no secret of the fact that the weak are wrong, their scruples are unnecessary and their consciences need enlightening with the truth. So long as these scruples are kept private and personal, they are tolerable and are not to cause friction in the church. But as soon as they are imposed upon others — as soon as weak Christians try to bind the conscience of the church with their own immature thinking — they are to be resisted.

## Decisions and marriage

Few decisions are more complex than choosing a marriage partner from within the vast pool of legitimate possibilities. Given that God made marriage as a covenant of companionship for life, factors such as personality, education and culture should not be ignored. Married partners need to complement one another if their marriage is to work well. But compatibility is far too complex an issue to be reduced to simplistic ideas of shared hobbies, political ideologies and careers. The differences between partners are often as important as the similarities. Who can possibly describe what really attracts two people to each other? The 'chemistry' of human love defies any clinical analysis. If ever 'feelings' play a large and valid role in decision-making they certainly do in marriage. There is nothing inherently wrong with that. Such feelings are unavoidable. God made us to have, and express, feelings towards one another. But as always, what we feel has to be held in check by the objective facts of divine revelation (rightly understood). The problem is that Scripture can be misapplied even when the intention is good. Take Genesis 24:12-20 for example, a text that has suffered from misuse in marriage guidance.

At first glance this text seems to support the reality of knowable divine guidance outside Scripture and the validity of devising a circumstantial test ('putting out a fleece') to discover God's will. Abraham wanted a wife for his son Isaac and he made his trusted servant responsible to find her. At a well near the city of Nahor the servant sought divine guidance: 'O LORD, God of my master Abraham, give me success today, and show kindness to my master Abraham. See, I am standing beside this spring, and the daughters of the townspeople are coming out to draw water. May it be that when I say to a girl, "Please let down your jar that I may have a drink," and she says, "Drink, and I'll water your camels too" — let her be the one you have chosen for your servant Isaac. By this I will know that you have shown kindness to my master.'

As the record shows, Rebekah fulfilled all the requested conditions and became Isaac's wife. Is that a model for us to use? Does that keep feelings in check and simplify the complex matter of choosing the 'right' person to marry? For both theological and practical reasons the answer is in the negative. This text is *descriptive* not *prescriptive*. It describes an unusual providence. It does not prescribe the normal marriage situation. It is not a paradigm. This is not the way

God normally works. This case was unique because of God's covenant with Abraham.

For God to keep his promise of numerous descendants for Abraham (Genesis 15:5), he would obviously have to have a son (Isaac), who in turn would need a wife to continue the covenant community. Isaac is not typical of 'any man' seeking a wife. He is the direct heir of the Abrahamic covenant. The fulfilment of God's covenant promise depended on a fertile wife for Isaac. That makes the event unique. That is not the situation for anyone today.

That is why both Abraham (24:7) and his servant (24:27) specifically refer to God as the one who is faithful to his promise. Moreover the text twice indicates Abraham's assurance of special guidance for the servant: 'The Lord, before whom I have walked, will send his angel with you and make your journey a success, so that you can get a wife for my son from my own clan and from my father's family' (vv. 7 and 40). How did Abraham know this? God must have revealed it to him. We are not in that position. None of us today has the assurance of angelic assistance in choosing our marriage partner.

Even at a purely pragmatic level this text is not a model to emulate. Which father or mother would seriously be prepared to consider sending out a messenger to find a spouse for their son or daughter? Who would then seriously regard that messenger's choice as being wisely made on the basis of something as mundane as a drink of water? Decisions about marriage can only be reduced to such simplistic models at the expense of both the integrity of Scripture and the practicalities of life.

## Decisions and gospel ministry

Should I become a foreign missionary or a preacher? The complexities faced by people considering missionary or pastoral service are very familiar to this writer. My decision to enter theological college to train for pulpit ministry was one of the biggest I have made. Since then I have helped many other Christians to work through the same issues. It has been a privilege to interview, assess, teach and examine candidates for various Christian ministries. Many went on to pastoral or missionary appointments, but not all. The church's wise sifting process made it clear to some candidates that other work was more consistent with their gifts.

Whatever the outcome, there was a feeling common to virtually all candidates. They felt that God wanted them in gospel ministry. They all had an inner desire to serve God as a minister or missionary. That subjective feeling often dominated every other consideration. For many it was interpreted as 'the call of God'. They were convinced it was divine guidance. It was held so intensely by some that they could not cope with a church or missionary board coming to a different opinion. How should we assess this? I will focus my comments on pulpit ministry but the same principles apply for missionary service.

There is certainly a subjective side for those contemplating pulpit ministry. God has made us very complex psychosomatic beings. There is an inward side to the Christian faith for all God's people. It must never be irrational (contra-objective), but it may exceed rational expression. It may go beyond our ability to analyse objectively. The danger comes when the experience of one or more saints is held out as the norm for all. This has happened in the development of the idea of 'a call to the ministry'. Some saints have apparently had strong subjective yearnings for the pulpit. But that has given rise to an entrenched tradition.

It has been made the rule and norm for others. Everyone applying for the pulpit is required to have a similar subjective encounter with God. It is expected to be similar in timing (prior to the pulpit), similar in intensity (a yearning that will not be satisfied with any other vocation) and similar in clarity (specifically interpreted as 'the call of God'; extra-biblical revelation, in other words).

Undoubtedly the Lord works wonderfully and mysteriously in the souls of men, communicating himself and his graces directly to us. We believe in this 'experiential' faith or 'experimental' faith, as some call it. We believe without question that God's Spirit does embrace his beloved people in wonderful encounters, lifting us up on wings of eagles, exhilarating us with an extraordinary sense of his powerful presence. I assume that when the divine Paraclete and glorious third person of the Godhead draws near to succour needy saints, they are well aware of 'the everlasting arms', even if words fail.

God's embrace may occur with or without secondary means. For example, he may refresh our inner man by means of a new insight into a scriptural text, or by an act of his providence. But he may also witness directly with our spirits, assuring us that we are his children (Romans 8:16). It would be unwise to prescribe or limit the modes by which God provides this subjective ministry. All these things we rejoice in, but none of it should be mistakenly called a revelation of the will of God.

> Subjective things have their proper roles but determining the mind of God is not one of them.

We must come back again to *sola scriptura*. Whenever the question is asked, 'What rule has God given to direct us how we may glorify and enjoy him for ever?' we reply with the Westminster divines. 'The word of God, which is contained in the scriptures of the Old and New Testaments, is the only rule to direct us how we may glorify and enjoy him' (*Shorter Catechism*, No. 2). Scripture is the *only* rule telling us the mind of God regarding men for the pulpit or any other gospel ministry. Subjective things have their proper roles but determining the mind of God is not one of them.

It is an undisputed fact that God gives preachers to his church, but what does that mean? How does that apply to candidates for gospel ministries? The following verses are typical of those commonly used to support the notion of an inward call of God: 'And how can they preach unless they are sent?' (Romans 10:15); 'Ask the Lord of the harvest, therefore, to send out workers into his harvest field' (Matthew 9:38); and 'Keep watch over yourselves and all the flock of which the Holy Spirit has made you overseers' (Acts 20:28). Also Ephesians 4 teaches that Christ, the risen and exalted head of the church, gives some as apostles, some as prophets, some as evangelists, and some as pastors/teachers.

It is reading far too much into those texts to assume that Christ has directly communicated with these gifted people, telling them they are raised up for one specific purpose in the eternal decree, namely, to be thrust out into the harvest as preachers. It is one thing to know that all validly appointed overseers have their ultimate authority from the Holy Spirit, but it is quite unwarranted to imply that such knowledge is to be gained privately before being appointed. Paul also argues that God provides other gifted people for the benefit of the whole body: servers, encouragers, helpers, givers, leaders, governors and givers of mercy (Romans 12). Why don't we expect them to have an inward sense of call? Restricting it to the preaching ministry is unwarranted special pleading.

Christians are free and responsible to serve God in any legitimate 'calling' consistent with their gifts. There is a large area of freedom. The same is true for men with preaching gifts. They have a free vocational choice. Some will choose the pulpit. Others might teach at school or university, or serve in Parliament or write books. We do great harm by talking about the pulpit or mission field as 'full-time ministry' as if other Christians only served God part time.

We are not to 'baptize' mere feelings about Christian ministry as a divine call: 'If anyone sets his heart on being an overseer, he desires a noble task' (1 Timothy 3:1). These feelings (aspirations, desires) are ours, not God's. The text goes on to list important qualities, skills, gifts, graces and mature characteristics that are mandatory. Every candidate must be blameless in his family life, social life and spiritual life. He must have a tenacious grip on Scripture and not be a recent convert. He must be apt to teach.

It also follows that a Bible teacher needs sufficient academic abilities to succeed in the required theological studies. He needs to pass the scrutiny of those in the church who are competent to judge these matters. In every case realism and humility are essential: 'Do not think of yourself more highly than you ought, but rather think of yourself with sober judgement, in accordance with the measure of faith God has given you' (Romans 12:3).

No matter how fervently a man interprets his feelings and experiences as God's 'call', the Bible tells us otherwise. The Head of the Church has spoken quite plainly about the type of men he wants in the pulpit, and he has nothing else to add: 'Nothing at any time is to be added, whether by new revelations of the Spirit or traditions of men' (WCF 1:6).

It is invalid to appeal to the 'call' of preachers like Jonah or Jeremiah as models for today. In the age of its infancy the church had no liberty to choose her preachers. Whenever she tried to do so she ran into trouble. God personally imposed preachers onto the Old Testament church. They were his mouthpiece in the most direct sense. God revealed his will to them and they transmitted that revelation to the church. They could claim 'Thus says the Lord' in the most immediate sense.

But Christ brought the church out of infancy to maturity (see Galatians 3). The church is no longer under the strict formalistic supervision of the old covenant but has received its inheritance. God now holds the church responsible for selecting preachers. He no longer calls and appoints them for us. He expects us to choose suitably gifted preachers according to clear guidelines (1 Timothy 3; Titus 1). God's former ways of revealing his will have ceased. They are not models to be applied today. Would any presbytery take on a candidate like Hosea ... a man whose wife was a harlot, with children 'not pitied', 'not my people', and 'scattered by God'?

The only 'call' available to a preacher now is from a congregation inviting him to occupy its pulpit. But even that is not 'the call of God'. Every preacher has liberty to decline that call. That is not sin. But if it were 'the call of God' there would be no liberty. Saying 'no' to God is sin. Even a super-abundant supply of preaching gifts does not imply a man has a 'call of God' either. Like everyone else, he is free to serve God in the vocation of his choice.

When the New Testament talks about God's 'call' it never refers to calling men to the pulpit. Rather, it has two main emphases. First there is the *call* of God in the gospel. In the case of the elect this call is made effective by the irresistible grace of the Spirit (regeneration). Then there is the *calling* or vocation in which every Christian serves God. There is no separation of sacred and secular. Every Christian has the same call to serve God, none more than others, and none less than others.

> Every Christian has the same call to serve God, none more than others, and none less than others.

Let the church call suitably qualified men to the pulpit. Let the church also call them out of the pulpit and into the Professorial Chair or the Board of Missions. But let us describe it accurately as *the call of the church*. Because it is within the area of biblical freedom it is a divine calling. But so is the work of a Christian mother raising her children, and a Christian martyr burning at the stake!

May God enable us to exercise biblical prayer, reason, faith, wisdom, brotherly love, humility and self-denial, as we face the often-complex task of making good decisions in our service of the King.

## Questions

1. *'Our dietary choices must never become matters of gospel faith.' Is that a fair summary of Galatians 1:11-16?*

2. *According to Colossians 1:16-23, what factors distinguish high standards of personal discipline from legalism?*

3. *'The teaching of Jesus in Mark 7:14-23 demands an end to scruples.' Is that a reasonable conclusion?*

# 15. Summing it up

This book argues that mature guidance is all about the sufficiency of Scripture for all life's decisions. Everything God wants us to know about his will is either explicitly revealed in the Bible or logically implied by it. What that means (both practically and theologically) has been teased out in considerable detail in fourteen chapters. It will be useful to close with a summary of the key issues.

## What guidance is not

Guidance is not a search for divine messages outside the Bible. There is no extra revelation to look for. We have the whole counsel of God. While God does have a 'secret or unrevealed will' (his decree for every detail in the universe) it is not accessible to us. What God decrees is only known after it happens, but hindsight is not guidance. Even if we could see ahead into God's secret will, that would be no advantage. It only reveals what we will do. It does not reveal our moral duty (what we should do). Only Scripture reveals that.

Guidance is not something we 'feel', like 'feeling led', 'feeling a sense of peace', or feeling anything. Feelings are natural and unavoidable and they have a proper role, but discerning the will of God is not that role. Right guidance does not always feel good. Wrong guidance may feel pleasant. But feelings are simply feelings. There is always a great deal of mystery attached to feelings and experiences. Interpreting them as divine messages is fraught with danger.

We are not to turn mere happenings into divine guidance. Happenings are not hints from God. Guidance does not seek to manipulate information out of God. There is no warrant for 'putting out a fleece', not for Gideon or anyone else. It is merely a fantasy arranged in the human mind, and it puts God to the test.

## What guidance is

Responding to divine guidance means living consistently with the Bible (God's 'upfront' guidance), while constantly trusting his sovereign decree (God's 'behind the scenes' guidance). In the latter, God rules and overrules all things for the success of his covenant purposes and the good of his people. Though its details are unknown to us, knowing about its existence is a great comfort.

Good guidance requires knowing the Bible well, and using proper methods of interpretation and application. A high view of Scripture will not deliver anyone from the pitfalls of misusing it. It is essential that such facts as the literary genre, together with the historical, grammatical and contextual details, play their full part in correctly 'reading' the Bible. No part of the Bible can be interpreted to contradict any other part or the whole product. The essential unity of the sixty-six books must always be observed. Mistakes will also occur if the organic (progressive) nature of biblical revelation is not appreciated. God did not reveal all things at once or with equal clarity. Truths given in embryonic form in the Old Testament grow into full fruit in the New Testament. We are bound to take wrong guidance from the Bible if we treat all texts on a 'dead-level' plain, thinking (for example) that all laws governing members of theocratic Israel still apply to the Christian church.

It needs to be said that life can still be complex. Having a right view of guidance is a great blessing. It will save us from many burdens experienced by people looking for non-existent clues about the will of God. But some decisions are still complex and hard to make. That is especially true in many areas of life where Scripture leaves us with a great deal of freedom. There is no right or wrong choice within the perimeters of biblical liberty. Here our personal feelings (likes and dislikes) have a large bearing on our choices, and rightly so. We need to pray for wisdom, humility and discernment as we weigh up all the factors in decision-making. We have seen how reason and faith also have important roles to play, and how self-denial may require us to forego certain liberties for the sake of loving other people. All of us have to be aware of the possibility of decisions being driven by undesirable pressures like covetousness, lust, ambition and pride. Personal integrity is clearly a factor in guidance and decision-making, and each of us must answer to God for that. Finally, it is hard to improve on the *Westminster Shorter Catechism*'s summary of guidance (Q. 2):

> What rule has God given to direct us how we may glorify and enjoy him for ever? The word of God, which is contained in the scriptures of the Old and New Testaments, is the only rule to direct us how we may glorify and enjoy him.

# Appendix

# Recent views on dreams and prophecy

It is reasonable to expect an author to interact with current literature, especially if it differs from his own work. What follows is a brief response to two current writers, Stuart Robinson and Wayne Grudem. It is brief because this is not the place for a technical or comprehensive response. But, in the interests of credibility, it is better to recognize what others are saying than to ignore it. A brief response is better than no response, and it may encourage others to read and think more deeply.

## Dreams

Dreams are a major feature in Stuart Robinson's book *Mosques and Miracles*.[1] The problem is not his appraisal of Islam but his doctrine of revelation. On this issue he has clearly cast his vote against the doctrine of revelation embodied in the historic creeds. 'It is estimated that of Muslims turning to Christ in Africa, 42% of new believers come through the experience of dreams, visions, angelic appearances or audibly hearing God's voice' (p. 273). He claims that Jesus appeared to them, telling them to follow him.[2] Robinson accepts these experiences as divine revelations, and has some very terse criticisms for those who deny it. There are three possible responses: guarded acceptance, willing acceptance, and non-acceptance.

## 1. *Guarded acceptance*

People who accept the Reformed creeds often take this option. They do not want to abandon belief in the sufficiency of Scripture, yet they find it difficult to reject the numerous claims of God speaking in dreams. So they say: 'In the vast majority of situations I agree that new revelation is not necessary, but some situations are unique. Perhaps God provides new revelations where Bibles are scarce. The creeds are right for 99% of missionary situations but I don't want to limit God. I believe the sufficiency of Scripture is generally true, but I want to be open to any God-given experiences.' There are several problems here.

For one thing it is self-contradictory. The sufficiency of Scripture is an absolute truth incapable of degrees. Either the Bible provides God's full and sufficient revelation for us or it doesn't. The notion that Scripture is quite sufficient *sometimes* automatically means it is also quite *insufficient* at other times. The word 'sufficiency' becomes meaningless. We end up with the absurd confession: 'I believe Scripture is sufficient revelation except in those circumstances where it is insufficient.'

A second problem is that the creeds do not allow for exceptions. The only question to be settled is whether they are right or wrong. As we saw in chapter 8, many creeds speak with the same voice as the *Westminster Confession* on the cessation of revelation. If the creeds are right, none of the Muslim dreams are revelations from God, nor are any other alleged voices from heaven. But if the creeds are wrong on such a fundamental doctrine, where else are they wrong? Did the most eminent theologians of the past get it wrong? Did the godliest and most learned assemblies on earth repeatedly make a mess of the doctrine of revelation? That question demands our verdict. 'Guarded acceptance' seeks refuge in a halfway house that does not exist.

Worse, it tosses us back into the sea of subjectivity. The Reformation delivered the medieval church from this very thing. It was drowning in the ocean of mysticism and uncertainty. Once the door for private revelations is reopened the door to truth and certainty is shut. Every man then has his own private version of 'God told me'. Each man has his vision of Jesus or angels, each man hears voices, and each man is convinced God spoke. But it is all subjective, mere feelings and sensations. They cannot be tested or contested. If you allow it for just one converted Muslim you cannot refuse it for a thousand. If you accept that God spoke to a man in Baghdad, you cannot deny it to another man in Brisbane. In one fell swoop the foundation of the Reformation (*sola Scriptura*) has been denied.

## 2. *Willing acceptance*

This is the position taken in *Mosques and Miracles*. One of its many problems is that of inherent contradiction. It is quite ironic that Robinson accepts the validity of revelatory dreams knowing the entire error called Islam is based on precisely such a dream! He describes Muhammad's first 'revelations' from God, and how there was absolute certainty that he was called to proclaim a new religion (pp. 129-130).

Obviously Muhammad was wrong (and Robinson agrees). His dream was not a revelation but a nightmare (in more ways than one). His convictions are irrelevant. God did not speak to Muhammad that night. To believe otherwise forces you to say that Christianity is wrong, or the true God told Muhammad to start a false religion! So how does Robinson disallow Muhammad's dream? Since he allows modern Muslims to say 'Jesus is God because he showed me in a dream', how can he deny the original Muslim from saying 'Allah is God because he showed me in a dream'? How can Robinson choose between dreams? How can he judge between subjective experiences?

I assume it is because he treats the Bible as the supreme standard of truth. In practice he is forced to agree with the historic creeds. All human opinions, beliefs and experiences must be examined in the light of Scripture. Those that accord with God's Word can be judged legitimate otherwise they are illegitimate. So Muhammad's dream is not divine revelation. Why then does Robinson criticize Christians who apply the same biblical assessment to every other dream?

The criticism becomes particularly virulent on page 242. Scepticism for these alleged supernatural phenomena is attributed to a gross lack of faith: 'so bereft of faith as to be considered atheists if not in name then in practice'. Blaming our Western culture, Robinson's most trenchant comment deplores that 'Our tradition places importance on articulation of the logical reasons for faith based on Scripture' (p. 244). This is profoundly disturbing! In reality his complaint should be praise. To lament a logical Bible-based faith is to depart from 2000 years of orthodoxy, opening the door to sheer superstition.

Another example of the same inconsistency occurs on page 268. At a taxi rank in Northern Iraq on the morning of 17 February 2003, Ziwar (who converted to Christianity seven years earlier) was challenged by Abd al-Salam to revert back to Islam. When Ziwar refused, Abd al-Salam shot him with an automatic rifle. In his statement to the police he claimed Muhammad had appeared in a dream telling him to kill Ziwar.

I assume Robinson would deny the dream was divine revelation (though he doesn't explicitly say so). But how can he deny it? What is the only credible argument against every 'God told me' claim? Only the written word of God, which says, 'You shall not murder.' So we are forced back to the sufficiency of Scripture. Abd al-Salam's dream (if it happened) is godless and anti-biblical. If Robinson accepts the Bible's judgement of this one dream why does he not consistently agree that it judges all dreams?

## 3. Non-acceptance

The correct response to dreams and visions is to deny they are revelations. That does not mean they are from the devil or that they are inherently bad. And it does not deny that God may use such dreams in the process of salvation. God is pleased to use all sorts of human experiences (even very disturbing experiences) to awaken sinners. Men have been saved after dreaming of falling into a bottomless pit. It did not really happen but God used their imagination as an instrument to soften hard hearts to the truth of the gospel. There is no need to assume that people who become Christians through dreams and visions are spurious converts. Perhaps some are, but the Bible shows some 'conversions' will prove to be false no matter what the context. We need a proper assessment of dreams.

Dreams are simply common human experiences. They usually bear little resemblance to any sober reality. They are often bizarre and surreal. Being psychologically mysterious, they defy clinical explanation. They can be triggered by a host of causes not discernible even to the dreamer. There are no rules and no limitations in dreams. One man's dream is as meaningful (or meaningless) as the next man's dream. Dreams are just dreams are just dreams! They are no more (or less) significant than other human psychic experiences like hunches or the strange feeling of déjà vu when it seems you are reliving your own history. Because God is sovereign he can use any of these things to accomplish his purposes. But they are not divine revelations. They are not to be baptized with the status of inspiration. They are not to be interpreted as 'God told me' something. Consider an example.

A man dreams a shark is chasing him. As the beast closes in for the kill, his whole life flashes past the screen of his mind. The drama reaches fever pitch as the jaws snap shut around his torso and the ocean billows with his blood. Then he suddenly awakens and finds himself sitting upright on the bed. He is sweating profusely, his heart is racing and he is terrified. But he quickly gets a grip on reality again. He realizes it was only fantasy. There was really no shark chasing him. He has no gaping wounds and all his blood flows safely in his veins. It was totally unreal but it felt very real. That's how it is with dreams!

Yes, God could use the man's dream to convert him. As he reflects on his frightening vision, the Holy Spirit causes this man to face his mortality. He realizes he will die one day. He will be in far greater danger than any shark attack. He will stand guilty before the God who made him, loved him and provided for him, whom he has denied and defied all his life. He has no excuse and no hope. The dream has softened him to the gospel. He is now prepared to receive the truth and follow Christ, maybe through a message God will cause him to hear next week, or maybe through the gospel he has known and ignored from childhood.

If it is possible to dream about a shark it is also possible to dream of seeing Jesus or hearing God's voice. But that doesn't make any of it real. In every case it is a figment of the mind. It is unclear how and why dreams occur, but one thing is certain: it is a serious mistake to claim they are revelations from God. It is irrelevant how convinced a dreamer is that God spoke. All that was true for Muhammad but he was radically deluded. And all that is true for every major cult leader in history. They all believe God appeared to them but they are all wrong. That is the verdict of orthodox Christianity throughout 2000 years of history. That is why the acceptance of revelatory dreams is the shame and scandal of the modern church.

## Prophecy

Can a true prophet of God deliver an untrue prophecy?
Does the New Testament provide examples? Does God
give infallibly correct revelations to his prophets who then
incorrectly deliver those messages to the church? Can a true
prophet lead you astray? Could disobedience be the right
response to a true prophet? In short, is there such a thing as
fallible divine prophecy? Wayne Grudem would say 'yes' to all
those questions. He sets out the reasons in his book *The Gift of
Prophecy in the New Testament and Today.*[3]

Grudem's novel view[4] on guidance has certainly thrown
a spanner into the works, which cannot be ignored by any
reasonable study on 'divine guidance'. Why does he say those
things? Is his thesis correct? What is a reasonable response?

### 1. *Grudem's theory described*

Grudem's basic mistake is his attempt to do what is logically
impossible — trying to reconcile two mutually exclusive
views of revelation. The cessationist position (represented in
the Protestant Reformed creeds) says that revelation ceased
with the completion of the Bible. The opposite view (which
Grudem constantly calls the 'charismatic' view) strongly
denies cessation. It claims God continues to give revelation to
the church today as in former ages. So Grudem asks: 'Can a
fresh examination of the New Testament give us a resolution of
these views? Does the text of Scripture itself indicate a "middle
ground" or a "third position" which preserves what is really
important to both sides and yet is faithful to the teaching of the

New Testament? I think the answer to these questions is yes.' He then asks both sides to modify their views (pp. 17-18):

> I am asking that charismatics go on using the gift of prophecy, but that they stop calling it 'a word from the Lord' — simply because that label makes it sound exactly like the Bible in authority and leads to much misunderstanding ... On the other side, I am asking those in the cessationist camp to give serious thought to the possibility that prophecy in ordinary New Testament churches was not equal to Scripture in authority but was simply a very human — and sometimes partially mistaken — report of something the Holy Spirit brought to someone's mind.

This is rather naive. Neither side could agree to his request without completely surrendering its fortress. Charismatics actually believe they are receiving prophetic 'words from the Lord'. They certainly do not want to downgrade them to the status of 'partially mistaken human reports'! They cannot agree to being recipients of inferior 'revelation' lacking the essential qualities of words from God, namely, infallibility and divine authority. That would be the death and burial of charismatic claims.

On the other side, how could any cessationist accept such a theory? Holding to the historic Christian creeds we deny that fresh supplies of true revelation are being *accurately* delivered today. So how could we agree with Grudem that fresh supplies of true revelation are being *inaccurately* delivered today? How can we possibly accept that God has placed true revelation in the hands of such incompetent agents? Why doesn't the

Holy Spirit support modern prophets as he did with the Old Testament prophets, preventing human error mixing with the truth? What could possibly explain such a radical departure from God's established pattern of revelation? Grudem admits that the Holy Spirit did keep apostolic revelation free from all errors, so why not the New Testament prophets also?

Grudem is trying to reconcile the irreconcilable. Revelation has either ceased or it has not ceased. No amount of semantic modification to the words 'yes' and 'no' can bring them closer together. No matter how it is worded, *ceased revelation* means it is finished and *not ceased* means it continues. A careful study of Grudem's arguments, not only in his book but also in his *Systematic Theology* published four years earlier,[5] exposes serious flaws in his case. These have been capably challenged by scholars like O. Palmer Robertson[6] and F. David Farnell.[7]

Grudem's thesis hangs on his radical distinction between God's prophets in the Old Testament and those in the New Testament. He claims that the true successors of the Old Testament prophets are the New Testament apostles, not the New Testament prophets.[8] He says only the apostles spoke with infallible divine authority, like Moses and Jeremiah of old. But the words of the New Testament prophets were not inspired, not authoritative, and not necessarily correct. Their origin was always a true revelation from God, but due to mistakes made by the prophet when he announces it to the church, accuracy cannot be guaranteed. This fallible announcement of an earlier infallible 'revelation' is what Grudem calls 'prophecy'.[9] From his study of 1 Corinthians 13, Grudem concludes that 'Apparently the prophet *may not always understand* with complete clarity just what has been revealed to him, and at times *may not even be sure* that he has received a revelation' (p. 102, his emphasis).

Grudem argues (from Acts 21:4) that the church could quite rightly disobey the prophecy. He asserts (from 1 Corinthians 14:29) that the whole congregation was duty bound to carefully sift out the true parts from the untrue parts of every prophecy. 'In 1 Corinthians 14:29 it seems that the prophet's words could be challenged and questioned, and that the prophet could at times be wrong. Yet there is no indication that an occasional mistake would make him a "false" prophet' (p. 69). This is a serious problem. We are asked to accept the existence of prophets whose messages are false, yet they are not false prophets! Grudem even argues (from 1 Corinthians 14:13-38) that there may be times when a prophet is so wrong that the congregation must entirely reject his prophecy.

It begs the question of why anyone would want to bother with something so faulty as the fallible gift of 'prophecy' Grudem describes. What church would want such a pool of mistakes? Wouldn't a mature church be better to stick with the truth, the whole truth and nothing but the truth (the Bible alone) as its source of divine guidance? What could possibly motivate Grudem to promote this faulty product? What is the advantage of having fallible prophets as well as mere preachers of the Bible?

The answer is found ... in the fact that prophecy is based on a divine 'revelation'. Because of this revelation, the prophet would be able to speak to the specific needs of the moment when the congregation assembled. Whereas the teacher or preacher would only be able to obtain information about the specific spiritual concerns of the people from observation or conversation, the prophet would have in addition the ability to know about specific needs through 'revelation'. In many cases the things revealed might include the secrets of people's hearts (cf. 1 Corinthians 14:25), their worries or fears (which need appropriate words of comfort and encouragement), or their refusal or hesitancy to do God's will (which need appropriate words of exhortation) (p.128).

But the problem is we can never know what God allegedly revealed to the prophet! All we have is what the prophet tells us but, as Grudem admits, you cannot rely on that. He might get it wrong. He can misunderstand or misrepresent or misapply what God really intended, so we have no way of being sure what to believe. There is no way of testing it. That evokes an obvious cry: *Give me a Bible preacher any day!* At least I can be quite clear if he makes an error. I have a written copy of the revelation he is explaining (the Bible) and I can test him against it! Grudem's theory throws us right back into the sea of subjectivism. First the prophet says, 'I think God said'. Then Grudem allows others in the church to say, 'I don't think you got it right.' But no one has any way of proving his point. We are virtually reduced to the options of superstition (believe anything) or scepticism (believe nothing). Neither of them is the biblical option, but of the two, scepticism has more credibility.

## 2. *Grudem's theory denied*

Grudem places much weight on two interpretive details, namely, his opinion that the prophecy of Agabus (Acts 21:10-11) was factually wrong in two respects, and his claim that the whole congregation evaluated the words of New Testament prophets (1 Corinthians 14:29). Edmund Clowney and others provide significant challenges to Grudem's exegesis on both these points.[10] In particular, Clowney shows how Acts 28:17 provides an accurate fulfilment of the Agabus prophecy. Interested readers should carefully work through the arguments to form their own judgement, but one broad perspective is worth noting here.

Even if we all agreed there are some difficulties interpreting Agabus, the only safe way to proceed is by preserving tried and trusted principles. Whatever the words of Agabus mean, they have to harmonize with the rest of Scripture. So far Grudem agrees, but then a basic problem in his methodology emerges. If the effort to demonstrate biblical harmony involves departing from the historic consensus of good exegesis, alarm bells should be ringing. Grudem seems to have made that departure, setting off the bells. How is that?

First he argues that there is a radical distinction between God's prophets in the Old Testament (infallible) and those in the New Testament (fallible). This obliges him to show an example of the latter, leading to his novel views on Agabus. But it cannot end there because the church then needs a method for coping with the mixture of truth and error spoken by fallible prophets. Grudem finds that in his novel interpretation of 1 Corinthians 14:29. One cannot help sensing that Grudem is chasing his shadow at every step. The hermeneutical circle he builds might be a harmonious unity, yet somewhat removed from reality. It may be a self-consistent model for the author's thesis without being the thesis of Scripture. It is one thing to know that a plane can fly well, but whose air space is it in?

Technical details aside, it is helpful to apply the macro-test announced by Jesus: 'A good tree cannot bear bad fruit, and a bad tree cannot bear good fruit... Thus, by their fruit you will recognize them' (Matthew 7:17-20). If we grant Grudem's theory of fallible prophets functioning in the church, what are the fruits? Are they good or bad? That will tell us whether Grudem is right or wrong. Three of them are certainly bad, namely, the fruits of confusion, bondage and regression.

*a. The fruit of confusion*

Imagine yourself sitting in the congregation when a prophet comes to the microphone and declares that God has given him a revelation. According to Grudem this 'prophet' is about to 'speak to the specific needs of the moment ... speak about the secrets of people's hearts, their worries or fears, or their refusal or hesitancy to do God's will'. The prophet says that someone in the church has chosen a career path contrary to God's will for his life. He claims God has revealed to him that the person in question is a computer software designer. The Lord wants him to give it up and go to Bible college to train as a foreign missionary. Suddenly you realize that, as the only software designer in the church, he is speaking about you.

Most people would feel a lot of pressure here. They would feel obliged to do exactly what the 'prophet' says. After all, it is no trivial thing to receive a revelation from God about your personal life. You feel many sets of eyes gazing at you. The prophet sits down and everyone sings the last hymn ... 'Trust and obey, for there's no other way, to be happy in Jesus, but to trust and obey'. Feeling humbled and rebuked, but zealous to obey, you go home determined to resign from your job and enrol at Bible college. But then you remember something Wayne Grudem said.

You remember him describing this as 'ordinary congregational prophecy for which no absolute divine authority is indicated' (p. 90). You remember his caution that the words of a prophet might be wrong and 'should not be thought of as "God's very words", nor should the speaker preface his or her remarks with words that would give that impression, such as, "Thus says the Lord," or "Hear the words of God" — those statements should be reserved for Scripture, and Scripture alone' (p. 111).[11]

What utter confusion! What are you supposed to do about your job? Does God really disapprove of your career in computer software? How can you tell if this is God's will or just the mistaken words of a deluded man full of self-importance? It gets worse because then you remember something even more staggering that Grudem had admitted, something he already said in earlier chapters: 'Chapters 3 and 4 ... caution the prophet against claiming certainty that the very words are God's words. (In fact God can cause words to come to mind that he does not want us to take as his own words. For example, he may bring to mind words that we ... imagine another person saying to us)' (p. 100).

This is tragic! It bears no resemblance to biblical prophecy. Why would God use a 'prophet' to speak for him with words that God does not want people to take as his own words? God is not the author of such confusion.

## b. The fruit of bondage

Bondage occurs when God-given freedoms are removed. The previous example illustrates such a case. In choosing our career paths God gives us a great deal of liberty. As long as it accords with the Bible's broad ethical principles, we are free to choose any career that we are capable of doing. If a believer has gifts suitable for software designing, he is free to do it. He is also free to choose numerous other options. All that freedom is 'the will of God'. But as soon as a 'prophet' removes the freedom and insists on just one option (missionary service), bondage is the result.

This is very bad fruit. It manipulates people in an arbitrary way. It is a form of legalism. It contradicts the Bible, yet it is happening in churches all over the world. Men who claim to be prophets stand over congregations asserting that God has privately revealed to them new details of his will for certain worshippers. This is a revival of Gnosticism (the ancient sectarian error claiming superior knowledge for a select few). God does not grant freedoms in his written word only to take them away by a later prophetic word!

## c. The fruit of regression

Regression means going backwards, moving from advanced to elementary, from mature to immature things. In this age of jet planes and modern cars we describe regression as 'going back to the horse and buggy days'. Grudem's notion of New Testament 'prophecy' is quite regressive. He agrees that God's prophets in Old Testament times were absolutely reliable, infallible and authoritative. They spoke exactly what God wanted. Their words were God's words. They were right when they began their prophecies with the classic formula, 'Thus says the Lord'. To disobey the prophets was to disobey God. No mistakes happened between the receiving of revelations and their proclamation. It was always sinful to ignore or disobey the prophets, and false prophets were to be put to death.

However, Grudem thinks that has all changed. Now the 'prophets' of the church are quite fallible and do not necessarily speak God's words. That's why he argues that the whole congregation is duty bound to carefully sift out the true from the untrue parts of every prophecy. That's why he admits there may be times when a prophet is so wrong that the congregation must reject his prophecy entirely.

In this scheme, revelation has gone backwards from infallible to fallible, from trustworthy to dubious, from inerrant to errant. This is completely out of step with what Scripture reveals. In every way the new covenant arrangements are better than the old covenant arrangements. To put it vividly: 'Christ on the cross is better than the brazen serpent on a stick. Resurrection from the dead is better than exodus from Egypt. Baptism is better than circumcision, and inheriting the new heavens and new earth is better than possessing Palestine. In this context ... it would seem strange indeed if new covenant prophecy took on a form that was significantly weaker ... than its old covenant counterpart.'[12]

It was once a solemn thing to hear a prophet of God. He spoke the very words of God. The Holy Spirit carried him along so that he preached and wrote exactly what God wanted to declare. You could stake your life on what the prophet said.

But Grudem's scheme is something far removed. He describes prophets as prone to err and unable to truthfully say, 'Thus says the Lord.' You cannot stake anything on their words. You may have to disobey what they say. They can be a complete waste of your time. In reality, you are far better off without them! A new hymn is needed: 'Backward Christian soldiers, backward from before, what the prophets tell us, no one can be sure'.

Can a true prophet be wrong? No, but a true Christian (like Wayne Grudem) can be wrong about the prophets. Undoubtedly he has spoken out of the noble motive of making peace. But there are times when pouring oil on troubled waters only pollutes the environment, creating worse problems.

# Notes

## Chapter 1

1. For typical examples of this model, see *Every Life A Plan of God*, J. Oswald Sanders (Grand Rapids, Discovery House, 1992), and *The Secret of Guidance* by F. B Meyer (New York, Fleming H. Revell Co., 1896).
2. I have adapted this illustration from *Decision Making and the Will of God* by Garry Friesen and J. Robin Maxson (Portland Oregon, Multmonah Press, 1980), pp.165-7.

## Chapter 2

1. See *Joni* by Joni Eareckson (Zondervan, 1976) and *A Step Further* by Joni Eareckson Tada and Steve Estes (Pickering & Inglis Ltd, 1978).

## Chapter 4

1. To illustrate this truth, Jay Adams contrasts providential circumstances with cans of sardines. Since the cans come with a key attached, opening them is a simple matter. But daily events are not like cans of sardines. They do not come with a key that allows

us to open (interpret) them. Providential circumstances require an outside key held by God alone. See *Guidance in Counselling*, by Jay E. Adams, 1996 (Michigan City, Ind.: Sound Word Associates, NANC Tape Library) as cited in *Step By Step: Divine Guidance For Ordinary Christians*, by James C. Petty (P & R, New Jersey, 1999), p.172.

2. Missionaries on the field often describe various 'wide open doors' (opportunities) that they can't possibly enter. So they plead for helpers to go and reap the harvest. It is good to pray that God would 'open doors' (as Paul does in Colossians 4:3). It is not a prayer for hints and revelations from God, but for opportunities to spread the gospel.

3. If we let the clear principles of Scripture interpret this incident, we have to conclude that Gideon erred here. He was wrong to do this thing, putting God to the test, seeking a miraculous sign. Firstly, God's directions had already been plainly given. The Lord had appeared and spoken directly, 'I will be with you and you shall defeat the Midianites as if they were just one man' (6:16). That plain word of God should have been enough. It needed no confirmation. In any case Gideon has already had it confirmed by a sign (16:17). He knew it was God talking to him.

Secondly, Gideon did not keep his word anyway. At first he told God he'd be satisfied with one proof (if the fleece alone was wet): 'then I will know that you will save Israel by my hand just as you said' (6:37). God graciously condescended to that request — but Gideon went back on his word and asked for yet another miracle — the previous one in reverse. He broke an assurance given to God. That is bad. Guidance comes from God's word, which, in Gideon's case, gave him no choice. There was one single thing to do, leaving no need for seeking further guidance. For us, Scripture often leaves a wide number of options — where to work or live, who to marry, what career path to follow. There is a lot of freedom. So long as we keep to the revealed word of God, acting according to its general principles, we are free to choose any one of the many options. We cannot go wrong if we stay consistent with Bible truths.

But we are not to be 'putting out fleeces' like Gideon. It is true God co-operated here. But God's gracious condescension to an erring child is not his stamp of approval! The Lord often blesses our mistakes because he is forbearing and patient, but it is no argument for the mistake. God knows we are feeble like dust, so he pities us as frail and erring children. But that is no excuse for doing feeble, childish things. There is no avoiding the fact: 'It is an evil and adulterous generation that seeks after signs' (Matthew 16:4).

## Chapter 5

1. The fact that Jonah happened to be at the pier at just the right time, with the right money in his pocket, and found a boat going in the direction he wanted to go, was mere coincidence. He was running away from God and his decision was still wrong.

## Chapter 6

1. *The Epistle to the Romans*, John Murray (New International Commentary on the New Testament, Eerdmans, Grand Rapids, 1968), p.159.

## Chapter 12

1. This infallible harmony refers to the original autographs. Obviously it is possible for translations (copies) to vary from each other and from the authentic originals as preserved in the Hebrew and Greek manuscripts. The science of textual criticism aims at defending the authentic text of Scripture.
2. Pope Leo XIII in 1893, quoted in *The Westminster Confession of Faith for Study Classes* by G. I. Williamson (P & R, Philadelphia, 1964), p.18.

3. Cited in *The Four Major Cults* by A. A. Hoekema (Eerdmans, Grand Rapids, 1963), p.227.
4. It is also seen in Barbara Thiering's 'Pesher Technique' which reinterprets Jesus as the wicked priest of the Dead Sea community, not the Son of God.

**Chapter 13**

1. Dr Clifford Wilson M.A., B.D., PhD. taught at Monash University in Melbourne and was a former director of the Australian Institute of Archaeology. He wrote more than seventy publications, including *The Stones still shout, New light on the Gospels, Crash go the chariots* and *Crash goes the Exorcist*. It is difficult to understand why he gave his support to Larry Mitcham's Bible Code.
2. Tragically this nonsense is merely a modern form of the old 'mechanical dictation' theory. In effect it sees Moses and the Prophets as mere typewriters punching out words (and multiple layers of coded words beneath the actual words) as the Holy Spirit drove them! It removes the vast bulk of meaning (all history) from the original writers. It disengages their brains and minds from their writings. Only the minute fraction of reality on the 'surface text' was their deliberate work. The vast untapped reality was in code.
3. Then he marvels at how the centre of this cluster was in the Song of Solomon 2:10, which says, 'My beloved spoke, and said to me, rise up my love, my fair one, and come away.' But if you feed a lot of marriage words into a computer wouldn't you expect a big strike rate in the very book that is all about the love of a husband and wife?

**Appendix**

1. *Mosques & Miracles: Revealing Islam and God's Grace* (Stuart Robinson, City Harvest Publications, Australia, 2004).
2. *Ibid*, p.263.

3. *The Gift of Prophecy in the New Testament and Today* (Wayne Grudem, Crossway Books, Illinois, Revised Edition 2000).
4. In his preface to the 1997 reprint (on pp.13-14) Grudem actually denies that his view is novel, claiming that some of the Puritans (including Samuel Rutherford and Richard Baxter) held the same opinion. Of greater concern is Grudem's attempt to call the *Westminster Confession* on side. He equates the 'private spirits' in WCF 1:10 with the 'private informative revelations from the Holy Spirit' that his thesis supports. Since the WCF insists all 'private spirits' are to be judged by Scripture alone (like all other opinions of men) Grudem sees them as essentially analogous to the fallible prophecies he describes. However that notion will not stand up under scrutiny, as demonstrated by Garnet Milne in the *Westminster Theological Journal* (Spring 1999, Vol. 61, No. 1). Milne is challenging Byron Curtis for his view that 'private spirits' in the confession means genuine 'private revelation' rather than mere private opinions (*Westminster Theological Journal*, 1996, Vol. 58), pp.257-99.
5. *Systematic Theology,* Wayne Grudem (IVP & Zondervan, 1994).
6. See *The Final Word,* O. Palmer Robertson, Banner of Truth, Edinburgh, 1993, pp.85-126. Dr Robertson taught for twenty years at the Reformed Theological Seminary, Westminster Theological Seminary and Covenant Theological Seminary. At the time of writing he served at the African Bible College, Malawi.
7. See *Fallible New Testament Prophecy/Prophets? A critique of Wayne Grudem's Hypothesis* (F. David Farnell, in *The Master's Seminary Journal* 2:2, Fall 1991, pp.157-79). Dr Farnell is Associate Professor of Biblical Studies at Southeastern Bible College. A PDF version of his critique is located at <http:/www.tms.edu/tmsj2h.pdf> (the html version is also available).
8. Grudem's interpretation of Ephesians 2:20 in defence of this view turns out to be a grammatical error. He has misused what is known as Granville Sharpe's rule (the rule that applies where two nouns

connected with the conjunctive 'and' (kai) are governed by only one definite article). For a more detailed explanation of Grudem's mistake, see Farnell's critique (*op cit*), pp.163-70.

9. Grudem, *op cit*, p.110.

10. For example, see *The Church* by Edmund Clowney (Downers Grove, Illinois, IVP, 1995) and an earlier work by Richard Gaffin, *Perspectives on Pentecost* (Phillipsburg, N.J., P & R, 1979). Grudem acknowledges and interacts with both of them in his book. For instance, see his response to Clowney in Appendix 4 (pp.307-11).

11. He quotes others with approval who say: 'Prophecy can be impure — our own thoughts or ideas can get mixed into the message we receive … there can be a whole range of degrees of inspiration, from the very high to the very low' (p.91).

12. *The Final Word*, O. Palmer Robertson, Banner of Truth, Edinburgh, 1993, p.97.

# *Also in this series...*

## WHAT THE **BIBLE** TEACHES ABOUT

# A N G E L S

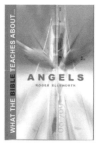

ANGELS in movies, television shows, figurines, books, magazine articles and seminars — angels are everywhere!

This would seem to be very good news. After all, the Bible does have a lot to say about angels, mentioning them 273 times. Should we not welcome such widespread interest in a biblical topic?

Yet interest in a biblical topic is of no value if we are not biblical about the topic. All too often, the only connection between the current angel-mania and the Bible is the teaching that angels exist.

In this straightforward and easy-to-read book in the What the Bible teaches about... series Roger Ellsworth sets the record straight, putting the biblical view of angels in a clear and helpful way, dealing with such topics as what are the seraphim and cherubim, angels as ministering spirits, and the role of angels at the beginning and end of time. Above all, however, is his concern to drive us to the one the angels themselves adore — the Lord Jesus Christ.

Roger Ellsworth, Evangelical Press, 128 pages,
ISBN-13 978-0-85234-617-4    ISBN 0-85234-617-4

A wide range of excellent books on spiritual subjects is available from EP Books. Please write to us for your free catalogue or contact us by e-mail.

EP BOOKS
Faverdale North, Darlington, DL3 0PH, England

**web: http://www.epbooks.org**

e-mail: sales@epbooks.org

EP BOOKS USA
P. O. Box 614, Carlisle, PA 17013, USA

**web: http://www.epbooks.us**

e-mail: usasales@epbooks.org